Asian Women in Higher Education
shared communities

Asian Women in Higher Education
shared communities

Kalwant Bhopal

Trentham Books

Stoke on Trent, UK and Sterling, USA

Winner of the IPG DIVERSITY Award 2010

Trentham Books Limited
Westview House   22883 Quicksilver Drive
734 London Road   Sterling
Oakhill   VA 20166-2012
Stoke on Trent   USA
Staffordshire
England ST4 5NP

First published 2010

British Library Cataloguing-in-Publication Data
A catalogue record for this book is available from the British Library

ISBN: 978 1 85856 469 2

Designed and typeset by Trentham Books Limited and printed in Great Britain by Berforts Group Limited.

Contents

Acknowledgements

I would like to thank the forty-five women who participated in the study, who gave generously of their time and shared their experiences with me. I would like to thank the gatekeepers for their time and efforts in enabling me to gain access to the respondents and the university. I am grateful to my colleagues at the University of Southampton (School of Education) for their support in the research and writing of the book and also to colleagues at numerous conferences where earlier versions of the chapters were presented. Thank you to all the team at Trentham especially Gillian Klein for her support and her editing, which has made for a more readable and accessible text.

I am grateful to Janet Ramsdale and Jean Rattray for their continued friendship and support. Huge thanks to my parents and siblings for their confidence in me. And finally I am eternally grateful to my longsuffering husband Martin Myers for his patience, for reading earlier drafts of the chapters and of course his musical taste! And to my children Dylan, Yasmin, Deva and Sachin for making me realise how important the Academy really is.

Dedication

*For my mum Swaran Kaur Bhopal and
my dad Gian Chand Bhopal
Thank you*

1
Understanding accounts of Asian women in British society

The lives of Asian women living in the UK, like those of all women, are shaped by many factors such as their age, class, religion, language and ethnicity. I use the term Asian in a generic sense to identify women whose ancestors (their parents or grandparents) originated from the Indian sub-continent: from India, Pakistan and Bangladesh. The different trajectories of their lives highlights the diversity and differences *within* and *between* different Asian groups. So the terminology 'Asian women' cannot be a generalisable means to understand the experience of all Asian women in British society but only a starting point from which to focus on the varied lives of women who share a migratory background. Just as their lives reflect different stories, a parallel trajectory originates from within the Academy to shape their lives.

This chapter examines the historically situated discourses that have been generated by academics and in which my research is situated. It argues for the importance of using a Black Feminist methodology when trying to account for the experiences of Asian women and how they are constructed as 'other'. It outlines an approach to research methodology that specifically explores the notion of difference in relation to issues of 'race', gender, age and class.

Asian women in British society

Much of the early literature on women's experiences in society did not focus specifically on the experiences of Asian women. Their experiences were either rendered invisible or, if taken into account, examined from a negative perspective (Khan, 1979). Scholars examined the 'push' and 'pull' factors affecting Asian families who migrated from the sub-continent to the West

(Anwar, 1979; Watson, 1977). The major push factor was to improve the family's financial and social position. The major pull factors were the active encouragement given by the receiving society to immigrants through the prospect of a 'better life': participation in the labour market and improved educational prospects for their children. Much of the literature on Asian families concentrated on the fulfilment of role obligations and expectations towards kin members. Within these traditional roles, in line with expectations of the sub-continent, it was the women who were entrusted with the burden of carrying the family honour (Wilson, 1978).

The literature in the 1980s focused on Asian women's cultural and familial experiences where they were stereotyped as weak and passive and suffered arranged marriages through systems of patriarchy, particularly in the home environment (Wilson, 1984). Their experiences were presented as homo-genous and essentialist. Asian women were 'caught between two cultures': the East (home) and the West (British values and norms). In this perceived 'culture clash', young Asians growing up in Britain were subjected to two dif-ferent cultures that they could not reconcile. The notion was that there is only one 'British' culture and only one 'Asian' culture, and although this was clearly not the case, it fitted a popular imagining of migration patterns as a novelty within British society.

According to the notion of 'culture clash', young Asian women were confused and unclear about their own identities because they were made to grow up in a restricted family environment that promoted a submissive role for girls that was challenged by their schooling experiences of Western values based on freedom and independence. This stereotyped view of both Asian and Western cultural norms stressed the degree of conflict and confrontation that occurred when Asian and Western society met. This perspective did not examine differences within the Asian groups and the impact of gender, class and age.

Some writers in the 1980s began to examine the position of Asian women within a cultural and historical framework, thus challenging essentialist ex-planations (Brah and Minhas, 1985; Parmar, 1988). Asian women's ex-periences were recognised as being lumped together, with little or no attempt to analyse the differences *within* Asian groups and the intersections of gender, class, educational background and religion.

In the 1990s the writings on Asian women began to recognise the differences *within* Asian groups and to explore the experiences of particular Asian groups and women's experiences within them. This included specific work on Sikhs

(Bhachu, 1991; Drury, 1991) and Muslims (Basit, 1997) and the significance of religion in women's lives (Shaw, 1988). Studies also recognised the importance of young Asians retaining their ancestral language within British society as a means of retaining tangible and distinct links to their parents' culture (Stopes-Roe and Cochrane, 1990). Other work demonstrated how some young Asians were able to synthesise British cultural values with traditional values, to develop new cultural patterns of belonging (Ghuman, 1994). Later, the work of 'Black Feminists' attacked the literature on Asian women for providing an ethnocentric and hegemonic perspective which pathologised Asian women and their lives and families (Brah, 1996; Mirza, 1997). This gave way to debates around difference and diversity and interpretations of cultural practices from a western perspective.

Much of the recent literature on Asian women has moved away from focusing on issues of the family, marriage and culture, to examine women's position within popular culture in relation to fashion (Raghuram, 2003), film (Bhatia, 2003), Asian lesbian identity (Kawale, 2003) and the positioning of Asian women within the academy (Puwar, 2004). Ramji (2007) explored how inequalities of racism, sexism and social class interact in the lives of young Muslim women. This recent research epitomises the movement away from pathologising Asian women and their lives, towards examining them as women who are affected by a range of intersecting differences such as age, class, religion and sexuality.

Patriarchy and Asian women

Many writers have explored the notion of patriarchy in relation to Asian women's lives. Early feminist work on patriarchy examined it as a system which oppresses women, the definitions of patriarchy and the causes of patriarchy (Barrett, 1980). Radical feminists argued that men's patriarchal power is the primary power relationship in human society. This power is not just confined to the public worlds of economic and political activity but characterises all relationships between the sexes. Marxist feminists see the origins of patriarchy as inextricably bound up with class society. Either way, patriarchy is not considered derivative of economic power or class society and cannot be reduced to other forms of domination. It must be understood in its own terms.

It was Walby (1990) who developed the most comprehensive analyses of patriarchy. Much of the criticism of patriarchy theory was directed towards its tendency to universalise women's experiences and so, conceal other forms of oppression based on race and class. Concepts such as patriarchy can conceal divisions in society in much the same way as male perspectives have concealed the oppression of women (Collins, 1990). Black feminists criticised the concept of patriarchy, arguing that because of racism, black men do not benefit from patriarchal social structures in the same way as white men. Westwood and Bhachu (1988) pointed out that patriarchal relations are neither monolithic or static, but contextualised by cultural elements within which they interact, including the means available to minority ethnic women to contest and negotiate patriarchal relations. Consequently, white feminists have been cautious in their use of the term. Walby (1990) however, argued that patriarchy ultimately unites all women in a common sisterhood as differentially oppressed subjects, who have in common a disadvantaged relation to men and that it is precisely this unity which provides the force for resistance. She argues that far from being unchanging, patriarchal domination takes a number of different forms which are the product of particular historical situations.

In 2006 Wilson argued that over the last 30 years, patriarchal relations were shaped and reshaped in different ways by Asian communities in Britain. Patriarchy is not an autonomous system, patriarchal relations are those which work to subordinate and oppress women. Accordingly, patriarchal relations are experienced differently in different societies, for example in pre and post capitalist societies. Wilson analyses the British state's relationship with Asian societies and describes how gendered hierarchies are consolidated within communities through multiculturalism by enhancing patriarchal power within the family. Patriarchal power within Asian communities has been affected by Asian women's struggles against it, and this is reflected in their mobilisation and political organisation. Wilson (2006) emphasises patriarchal control of women's bodies, marriage, mental health and domestic violence, and the labour market. She argues that Asian women's needs cannot be addressed without reference to the racism they experience for instance in the labour market or their treatment by health services. In attempting to nuance understandings of Asian women's lives some writers have moved away from using the term patriarchy but focus instead on the experiences of Asian women in relation to their positioning in society, for example being a student, being middle class or being a member of a specific religious group (cf. Bhopal, 1997).

Much of the literature on Asian women's experiences has been descriptive and failed to examine the interrelationships between class, gender, race and age. It has failed to provide a theoretical understanding of women's lives, focusing on the negative aspects associated with cultural understandings of the different groups – for example the notion of 'forced' or arranged marriages. The experiences of Asian women in Britain are inextricably bound up with race, class, religion and region of origin and other diversities which shape and reshape their gendered and racialised experiences. Yet a significant body of research has presented essentialist and pathological accounts of the lives of Asian women and has failed to provide a theoretical understanding of their lives. This book examines how gender relations within Asian communities have undergone a major transformation, specifically in relation to women's experiences of their families and their communities and what this means within the context of their experiences in higher education. The research acknowledges the particular tensions and pressures faced by Asian women and argues that, within these complex modes of being, Asian women are re-defining what it means to be Asian in British society by using their education as a means of empowerment to instigate change in their lives.

This book draws on my research examining the experiences of Asian women in higher education, specifically in relation to issues around friendships, marriage, dowries, support and the importance of education in their lives. I sought to engage directly in a research process in which the race and gender of respondents was explicitly understood and valued. For many of the respondents the research provided a rare opportunity to reflect on their lives and the choices they were making compared to their mothers' and grandmothers' generation. The research thus not only gave voice to a group of women who have generally not had the chance to be heard, but also flagged up the lives of young Asian women who will have a greater say and greater visibility in British social life in the future.

A Black feminist methodology

My research uses a black feminist methodology in order to conceptualise the nature of the research and to provide a framework in which the differences of Asian women can be highlighted and valued. A feminist methodology is concerned with examining research from women's perspectives and valuing this from the point of view of women and researching women's lives in terms of giving a voice to respondents. Feminist critiques of research methodologies argue that methodologies of conducting research have a male bias.

Whilst it can be argued that there is no one way of conducting research within a feminist methodology, certain principles can be drawn out. These focus on the need for women's lives to be addressed in their own terms; feminist research should not just be about women but also be for women. It should consider how it might improve the lives of women. A feminist research methodology involves examining the research from a self-reflexive perspective, so that the researcher can be aware of the biases and perceptions they bring to the research process. Feminists are concerned with examining the research process as a political act; raising questions for example about the researcher's choice of topic, method and respondents and most of all asking how the research will make a difference to women's lives.

From this viewpoint, a feminist methodology and a feminist epistemology are required. The method provides the tools for conducting the research, the methodology provides the perspective and the epistemology provides the particular theory of knowledge and is concerned with what counts as knowledge. As Allen and Walker state, 'Feminism is a perspective (a way of seeing), an epistemology (a way of knowing) and an ontology (a way of being in the world)'. (1992:201). Feminist research differs from other types of research by its 'worldview rather than method' (Allen and Walker, 1992:201). Campbell and Wasco argue that the ultimate aim of feminist research is to 'capture women's lived experiences in a respectable manner that legitimates women's voices as sources of knowledge' (2000:783).

Feminism works to challenge the subordination and silencing of women. From this perspective women are encouraged to tell their stories in their own words. The focus of feminist research is a commitment to social change (Fonow and Cook, 1991). Research conducted within a feminist framework aims to construct knowledge which may benefit women by paying attention to issues of difference, questioning social power differentials and committing to political action and social reform (Byrne and Lentin, 2000).

The concept of difference has a long history in feminism. But difference was used to analyse how women were the same or 'different' from men, not to examine the diversity of women's experiences. The assumption that gender unites women more than other differences has been vigorously challenged by black feminists. Black feminist researchers have criticised the work of feminists for providing an ethnocentric viewpoint which does not take into consideration the position of black women and fails to examine how black women and their experiences are 'othered'. They argue that simple notions of women as a homogenous group who share a common oppression do not examine the complexity of women's lives.

Accepting that thinking must critically engage with meanings of difference and diversity created the need to question what difference and diversity meant within the project of 'feminist research' (Anthias and Yuval-Davis, 1992). Race infuses itself into the research process and the interview situation in much the same way that feminists argue that gender does. Race works to place the researcher and the respondent within the hierarchy of the social structure and can have bearings upon the relationship between the researcher and the researched, as we see below. Black feminists have been crucial in examining the meaning of feminism and how such a concept and discourse can be applied to the experiences of non-white women. Within studies on the family, for example, black feminists have highlighted how racism and sexism have been used to pathologise understandings of black families as well as influencing stereotypes of black femininity. White feminists have focused on the family as a key site of oppression for women, yet black feminists have shown that for many black people the family can be a key site for resistance and solidarity against racism (Carby, 1982; hooks, 1982).

Black feminists have also emphasised that oppression itself cannot be quantified and there is a danger that feminists may develop a hierarchy and competition of oppression in which some women are seen as more oppressed than others (hooks, 1982). Collins (1990) states that examining layers of oppression only obscures issues of difference. Such issues of diversity have been explored in relation to education by examining the experiences of Black girls in schools (Mirza, 1992) as well as the racism and sexism of teachers and viewing Black and Asian students as 'problem students' (Shain, 2003; Wright, 1987).

I use the tools and traditions of feminist methodology as a starting point for understanding the lives of women. This is necessarily and overtly nuanced by paying attention to the ethnic and racial dimensions that have affected and continue to affect the lives of Asian women.

Research methodology

Forty-five women participated in my research. All were studying at the same post-1992 university in the South East of England and were on Social Sciences or Education Studies degree courses. The women were recruited in the university via advertisements on noticeboards and year group announcements. Semi-structured interviews were carried out in private on university premises. The interviews were tape-recorded and the data transcribed. They took approximately 1-2 hours.

The respondents were informed of the project aims and objectives. Issues of confidentiality and anonymity were explained and the respondents signed a consent form to participate in the research. Most of them (39) wished to see their interview transcripts so they could change them if they wished, and all were given this opportunity.

The fieldwork took place in two phases. The first twenty interviews were held during the year 2004-2005 and the second during the year 2006-2007. Phase one respondents were in their first year when interviewed and phase two respondents in their third year. All were interviewed once. Respondents could withdraw from the study at any time without explanation, but none chose to do so.

The women were aged between 20-30. Sixteen described themselves as Hindu, thirteen as Muslim and sixteen as Sikh (see Appendix for details of respondents' backgrounds).

The data was analysed using methods of grounded theory as described by Strauss and Corbin (1990) and developed by Charmaz (2006). I used grounded theory analysis in the research, on the premise that systematic qualitative analysis has its own logic and so can generate theory. The process of data analysis included a simultaneous involvement in the data collection and analysis, constructing analytical codes and categories from the data, making comparisons during each stage of data analysis and examining the process of theory development through each stage of the process of data analysis. The aim was to move beyond descriptive analysis into an explanatory theoretical framework so as to provide conceptual and abstract understandings of the phenomena being studied.

I adopted a black feminist methodology to give voice to my respondents and let their voices be heard. The best way of conducting this type of research was to use qualitative research methods, as these are flexible, fluid and better suited than quantitative methods to exploring the understanding of meanings, interpretations and subjectivities of particular groups. Qualitative research methods allow researchers to hear the voices of those who are 'silenced, othered and marginalised by the dominant social order' (Hesse-Biber and Leavy, 2005:28). I took the view that qualitative research provides the researchers with an opportunity to listen to respondents tell their life stories (Warr, 2004). I wanted women to be able to share with me their lived experiences of being an Asian woman in British society.

I wanted to include my own experiences as a researcher and as an Asian woman, both in the conducting of the research and in the sharing of the respondents' subjectivities. Many of the respondents may well have been more comfortable speaking to me than to a non-Asian researcher about their experiences. They had a 'shared identity' and 'shared empathy' with me. I spoke to them about my own experiences of being an Asian woman in British society, of the experiences of my mother and sisters concerning arranged marriages and dowries and about my own experiences of racism.

The research provided the opportunity for me, the researcher, and the respondents to establish a relationship of trust and rapport. A conscious feminist methodology must explore the way in which the researchers can include their own experiences as women and as researchers, in both the conducting of research and the sharing of subjectivities with the participants (Moran-Ellis, 1996). As Moran-Ellis writes, 'the positioning of the researcher as a person who is gendered and has their own particular origins has come to be seen as an important, albeit often invisible, component in the research process' (1996:176). I also sought to be reflexive throughout the research process, by standing back and taking time to assess the research from a distance.

The research paid attention to notions of difference and diversity, examining the lives of those who are 'other/ed and marginalised' (Hesse-Biber and Leavy, 2005). Dunbar, Rodriquez and Parker (2002) argue that the researcher's self-disclosure is essential when carrying out research with minority ethnic groups. In particular, respondents whose voices are generally silenced and whose lives are othered may well regard the researcher and her association with an academic institution with suspicion. It can be important for the researcher to reveal something about themselves, to demonstrate a little more about their lives than just their academic and professional credentials in order that trust can be gained and rapport achieved. As Fontana and Frey state,

> It is paramount to establish rapport with respondents: that is, the researcher must be able to take the role of the respondents and attempt to see the situation from their viewpoint rather than superimpose his or her world of academia and preconceptions on them. (2005:708)

One means of a connection with respondents and thereby allowing greater understanding of their lives is to step away from the preconceived role of 'academic researcher'. Research itself is a process. It involves a journey and is concerned with the reasons why we do research as well as assessing the different issues involved, such as examining difference and diversity within the research process. This may include the notion of power differentials and how our race, age, gender and class may affect the research process itself. It was from this position that I based my research. I was aware of my positioning as an Asian woman researcher conducting research with Asian women and the advantages and disadvantages associated with this.

2

Communities and Identities

Communities

The concept of community is ambiguous, contested and has myriad meanings. Early work on community such as by Tonnies (1887) distinguished between *gemeinschaft* and *gesellschaft* relationships in traditional and industrial society. By *gemeinschaft*, Tonnies meant the sense of community that emerges within intimate face-to-face relationships, driven by the contingencies of social and geographical place; typically the belonging to a particular locality amongst family and friends. Tonnies portrayed *gesellschaft* relationships as much more superficial, impersonal and calculating, driven instead by the more competitive and highly mobile nature of industrial society. Such relationships are not an end in themselves but rather a means to generate profit and further self-interest.

What Tonnies is describing is the industrialised transition in the West from rural lifestyles to urban society and the adaptation of relationships within new economies that become far more specific. Unsurprisingly, he was pessimistic about the effects of industrialisation on society. He saw it as causing the death of the community, with dire consequences for social relationships: he probably foresaw much of the sentimentality that would mark popular discussions of what is meant by community and specifically what has been lost in the experience of community in the late twentieth and early twenty-first centuries.

Similarly, according to Beck (1992), modern society has generated new forms of individualisation, which can affect patterns of interaction in modern housing and living arrangements. Modern housing has replaced traditional settlement patterns and consequently traditional forms of community that once existed beyond the family are beginning to disappear. As members of families choose their own separate relationships and live in networks of their own, neighbourhoods become scattered and new social relationships and social networks are individually chosen. Social ties have to be established, maintained and constantly renewed by individuals. As a result of this change, '*self-selected and self-created hierarchies and forms of stratification* may develop in relationships with acquaintances, neighbours and friends' (1992: 97 original emphasis). These relationships are based on the interests, ambitions and commitments of individuals who, when they look in the mirror, see themselves as creating and allied to their *own* circles of contacts and relationships. Divisions between cultures and countercultures may therefore emerge at the same time as new forms of cultural and social identity develop.

In many ways the impact of such changes to the creation and establishment of relationships that distance individuals from more traditional support structures such as the family or local community has been to foster the desirability of a greater sense of belonging to a more traditionally understood community. Being a member of a community makes its members feel comfortable and ensures a sense of safety and security (Bauman, 2001). Those who are members of secure communities are envied in the modern world. As Bauman notes, 'Community is nowadays another name for paradise lost – but one which we dearly hope to return to and so we feverishly seek the roads that might bring us there' (2001:3). For all that the experience of community is ever more lost, the importance of understanding community as a societal building block has become ever more prevalent. Community has become a crucial concept in the analyses of friendship, ethnicity and faith and is one way of talking about everyday reality as an important source of collective identification (Jenkins, 2002:63). The concept of community has been discussed in relation to communitarianism (Etzioni, 1993), social capital (Putnam, 2000), anthropology (Amit, 2002) and empirical analyses of community (Keller, 2003).

If community – when understood in terms of change or of the relationships between different communities, or in the contrast between nostalgia for what has gone and cannot be recreated as desired – is an ambiguous term, other understandings seem more clear-cut. Redfield (1971) suggests it is clear who is 'one of us' and who is 'one of them', members of community know where they stand and there is no cause for confusion or ambiguity about belonging or not belonging. A community is distinct from other groups (it is clear where it begins and where it ends); it is small (the members know who is and who is not part of it) and self-sufficient (it provides for its members). The distinctiveness of the community is translated in the clarity of who belongs and who does not.

Community in its simplest form refers to a territorial sense (such as a neighbourhood, a city or a town) or a relational sense (such as a spiritual community or a volunteer or support group). In modern societies it has been argued that communities develop around interests and shared goals rather than around a particular place or territory (Gusfield, 1975). The concept of community can convey multiple meanings relating to where people live, how they live or the ways in which they may be distinguished by others (Reynolds, 2000). Individuals are connected to a sense of community when they experience a notion of belonging to a group in which they perceive themselves as similar (Sarason, 1974).

Part of this belonging is based on '...a feeling that members have of belonging, a feeling that members matter to one another and to the group, and a shared faith that members' needs will be met through their commitment to be together' (McMillan and Chavis, 1986:9). In this sense the members of the community will work together to develop strategies which are aimed at increasing a sense of community (Martini and Sequi, 1995). Community has a positive effect on group mobilisation to solve problems (Francescato and Ghirelli, 1998), enhancing quality of life and well-being while combating anonymity and loneliness (Chavis and Wandersman, 1990) and developing positive relationships between its members (Davidson and Cotter, 1991). As Weeks observes,

> The strongest sense of community is in fact likely to come from those groups who find the premises of their collective existence threatened and who construct out of this a community of identity which provides a strong sense of resistance and empowerment. (2000:240-3)

So we can readily understand Bauman's description of the longing for community:

> We miss community because we miss security, a quality crucial to a happy life, but the one which the world we inhabit is ever less able to offer and ever more reluctant to promise. (2001:144)

We all live in a world in which our longing for a sense of security seemingly reinforces our sense of insecurity and, whilst it would be trite to suggest we are all outsiders now, one construction that can be placed on feelings of insecurity is the disjuncture between individual lives and closeness to traditional community structures. However, it is perhaps the groups who remain outsiders who constantly strive to maintain and strengthen the cohesiveness of their community, thus conveying a greater sense of their place in the world and a means of surviving in it (Bhopal and Myers, 2008).

In *Imagined Communities,* Benedict Andersen (1983) examines the concept of 'nation' in relation to an imagined political community. He explores how the nation is imagined as limited, as sovereign and imagined as a community because of the inequalities and exploitation that exist within it. Andersen also explores the ways in which communities share membership through their language and how knowledge of language affects whether one can become a member of the community. In Andersen's imagined community, the strength of it is largely that it copes with change by *imagining* a structure, the nation state, to replace the lost communities.

Cohen (1985) examines the 'symbolic construction' of communal and other collective identities. He explores how individuals construct a sense of themselves and others as belonging in a particular locality or in the setting of particular relationships and interactions. His idea of community membership depends upon the symbolic construction and signification of our similarity. He maintains however, that the similarity of communal membership is imagined and seen as a symbolic presence in people's lives but that community itself is not imaginary. These similarities and differences reinforce boundaries which exist in communities. Cohen emphasised the symbolic construction of community in which symbols generate a sense of shared belonging, which may include shared rituals.

Within the community, communal boundaries are negotiable and shifting. Community can mean different things to different people, but what is important is not that members see or understand things in the same way but rather that their shared symbols allow them to believe that they do. As Cohen argues,

> ...culture – the community as experienced by its members – does not consist in social structure or in the 'doing' of social behaviour. It is inherent rather, in the 'thinking' about it. It is in this sense that we can speak of the community as a symbolic, rather than a structural construct. (1985:98)

Community is a symbolic construct based on boundaries and community membership and its boundaries symbolise both inclusion and exclusion. It is based on sharing with others a sense of community and participating in shared activities in which fellow members have shared symbols of their identity which will allow them to understand their sense of belonging within their community. Cohen offers a developed understanding of the relationship between boundaries of identification and what boundaries consist of within communities.

For young Asian women living in Britain whose identity is shaped by attachments to both Asian and British culture, to the world of their parents and of their peers we might anticipate understandings of community to be ambiguous. Although there is some truth to this, my research has identified some particular notions of community. A strong sense of community is one in which members are able to meet each other's needs at the same time as fulfilling their own. The fulfilment of needs is related to the shared emotional connection the members have to each other, based on a shared history of the group. It is not necessary for the individual to have played a part in the history, just that they can identify with it. These elements of community are interrelated. Viewed in this way, we can see the community as constructive: a positive force which enables its members to identify with each other through their shared histories.

The community has boundaries of membership which determine whether one can or cannot belong. Belonging is based on shared identity and shared history. Becoming a member of the community brings security and ensures a safety which enables women to share their sense of identity with other like-minded individuals. Communities are based on the notion of membership and the feeling that one is 'part of something', shared personal experiences and ties with others. Belonging relates to the definition of boundaries – to who is an insider and who is an outsider. The community offers the individual a form of emotional security, a form of identity and the sharing of a cultural system.

Communities of practice

The concept of a community of practice was introduced by Lave and Wenger (1991) and developed by Wenger (1998). Lave and Wenger (1991) suggested that individual members of communities learn by participating in shared activity, not merely in formal or institutional settings such as the workplace or university but also within a wider environment in settings such as the home, the local community and the workplace.

Wenger's (1998) social theory of learning is based on the premise that individuals are active participants in the practices of their social communities and can construct identities in relation to them. There are four central components (1991:5): *Meaning* – the way of talking about our experiences of the world; *Practice* – of how shared historical practices can become part of mutual engagement; *Community* – our participation in what we find meaning in. *Identity* – a way of talking about how learning changes who we are and how our personal histories are created within the context of our communities.

Wenger argues that communities of practice exist everywhere and are an everyday part of our society. Every individual belongs to a community of practice, but we can belong to more than one at any given time. Communities of practice are often taken for granted; they are informal and the types we belong to can change over the course of our lives. We know clearly who belongs to our communities of practice, yet membership is not made explicit. We are also aware of those communities of practice in which we have limited or peripheral membership. According to Wenger, a community has three fundamental aspects: mutual engagement, a joint enterprise and a shared repertoire.

Mutual engagement

The mutual engagement of the participants of a community is what holds the community together. One reason for a community's existence is because its members are engaged in actions in which the meanings of the community are negotiated with one another. 'Membership in a community of practice is therefore a matter of mutual engagement. This is what defines the community' (Wenger, 1998:73).

Joint enterprise

The negotiation of a joint enterprise is also a source of community coherence. The joint enterprise is based on the collective process of mutual engagement and defined by the participants of the community and how they respond to situations which they can or cannot control. The joint enterprise becomes an integral part of the practice in which all members are accountable.

Shared repertoire

A shared repertoire is the third aspect of community coherence. The repertoire of a community of practice includes particular ways of doing things: the words, language, gestures and symbols used. It is based on concepts that have been developed within the community of practice and which have become part of its practice.

Wenger argues that the existence of a community of practice does not necessarily depend on a fixed membership. Members can come and go and members can change at any time. An important part of the existence of a community of practice is the change in its members, through different generations. He maintains that the practice can be shared across different generations as it is already seen as having a fundamental role in the process of learning for the community. Communities of practice have boundaries of membership such as titles, dress and level of education to name but a few. Outsiders who do not identify with these markers of membership will be refused entry into the community of practice.

Communities of practice also involve boundary encounters – the meetings, conversations and events that may take place between the members. Each of these can take on a different purpose, but each will also have specific boundary definitions as to who is and who is not part of the boundary encounter. The practice of boundary encounters is what connects the members of the community of practice. They develop particular ways of communicating and engaging with each other, which outsiders may be unaware of or unable to enter into. The members understand the shared enterprise and develop a shared repertoire which is unique to its members. The boundaries are used to keep insiders in and outsiders out. The emphasis is on a shared understanding between the members of a community of practice.

Wenger argues that communities of practice can connect with the rest of the world by providing some kind of peripheral experiences, including observation. Individuals who have this role are neither inside nor outside the community. They maintain a peripheral role. The community is constantly negotiating and renegotiating the relationships between the core members and those on the periphery. 'Boundaries and peripheries refer to the "edges" of communities of practice, to their points of contact to the rest of the world, but they emphasise different aspects' (Wenger, 1991:118).

Belonging

Within the processes of identity formation and learning, there are three different modes of belonging. Firstly, there is *engagement* which is based on the negotiation of meanings; secondly, there is *imagination* which allows connections to be seen though time and space based on their own experiences; and, finally, there is *alignment* that is coordinating our own activities to fit in with broader structures. Essentially it is through processes of engagement that communities of practice are formed and later that individuals can use imagination to disengage from their communities of practice so that the practices of the communities can be re-invented and take on new meanings. Alignment is based on having common purposes and then being able to link these to broader discourses of meaning.

Identity

Engaging in a community of practice gives members a shared sense of identity. But many individuals might not deal with their issues of identity in a direct fashion; they might not, for example, be willing to talk openly about their identity. The individual's identity is still something that forms part of their community of practice and is of great importance to how individuals relate to each other. Thus 'the formation of a community of practice is also the negotiation of identities' (Wenger, 1991:149). Wenger identifies five different aspects to the formation of identity within a community of practice.

1. *Identity as negotiated experience* – we define who we are by the ways in which we participate in our communities of practice.

2. *Identity as community membership* – we define who we are by those things, which are familiar and unfamiliar to us.

3. *Identity as a learning trajectory* – we define who we are by where we have been (our past) and where we are going (our future).

4. *Identity as a nexus of multimembership* – we define who we are by the ways in which we are able to reconcile our different forms of membership into one identity.

5. *Identity as a relation between the local and global* – we define who we are by negotiating local ways of belonging to broader styles and discourses (1991:149).

Identities are closely bound to the trajectories, that is to say to the connections between the past, present and future that exist for individuals within and across different communities of practice. Different types of trajectories exist within communities of practice. These include: *peripheral trajectories*, which may not necessarily lead to full participation in the community of practice; *inbound trajectories*, by which new members will join the communities of practice at different times and may become full members; *insider trajectories*, in which the formation of identity is an ongoing process; *boundary trajectories*, which link communities of practice and work across different boundaries of membership; and *outbound trajectories*, which may be based on finding different positions with respect to the community of practice (Wenger, 1991:153).

Asian women's trajectories

In my consideration of Asian women who are studying at University, I found that their ideas of belonging were related to their ideas of safety in a world in which they felt marginalised and different. Frequent face-to-face communication influenced how members perceived the community. Having regular meetings, which were generally informal, such as sharing coffee breaks in the canteen, meeting in the library, sitting together in lectures and seminars or having lunch together, positively reinforced the membership of their communities within the university setting and the effectiveness and collaboration which existed within it.

This was an ongoing process in which the women were members of the same community of practice for a period of two to three years. The ongoing communication helped reinforce the shared practices within the communities. Cultural and religious beliefs generated a shared understanding between the women and this was also based upon the women being part of a minority ethnic group, one which had similarities and differences, but which was essentially seen as being 'different' from other, more dominant groups within the university. It was this notion of 'otherness' that encouraged them to become friends with Asian women regardless of their religious background.

The various trajectories of their identities was complex, multi-layered and changing. Within the home environment they had a particular identity they were keen to adhere to, based upon cultural norms and rules of behaviour. Within the university environment this identity changed and was based on how they defined themselves in relation to others. The women felt connected to other Asian women within the university environment, being included within a group through mutual engagement and an acceptance of their identity and cultural background as *Asian women*. Within their community of practice, Asian women could engage with other women, acknowledge each other as participants, and have a clear understanding of each member and the negotiation of their identities. Despite complex individual identities that required many of them to negotiate a multifaceted cultural environment with some dexterity, they had a shared understanding of each other's complex lives. It is this clear membership of the community of practice which helped shape the meanings that defined the community and forms of belonging for Asian women. As Wenger notes, 'communities of practice can be thought of as shared histories of learning' (1998:86).

Being part of the community of practice enabled the women to feel respected and accepted. They could identify with others within the group. Being included within the community was part of their engagement within it, just as being engaged within the community was part of *belonging* to the community. Women's communities of practice were defined by their past – their Asian culture and upbringing – as well as their future – their participation in

Asian events such as marriage and social functions. It was these *histories* and *futures* which bound women together in their communities of practice. Many saw their own future identities as *British Asian* women. They were clear that their identities as British Asian women were very different to the identities of their mothers.

Women's identities are constantly changing and in a state of flux. They are negotiated and re-negotiated according to where they are and who they are with. Asian women in higher education are engaged in communities of practice in which they identify themselves through language, dress and a cultural awareness and understanding of each other's background. Education was used as a means of self-empowerment. The community in which Asian women are engaged is active, engaging and informal. Asian women experience not only a 'shared understanding' but also a 'shared identity' within the university environment.

The informality of the communities of practice encouraged voluntary membership as the informal atmosphere encouraged the members of the community to share their knowledge and beliefs (Wenger, 1998). It has been argued that this informality is the main advantage for such communities, as it strengthens cohesion for its members (Wenger and Snyder, 2000). For many of the women, being engaged in communities of practice included forms of mutual engagement which were based on shared identities in which meanings and discourses were negotiated, defined and redefined.

Asian women define who they are through the familiar and the known. This takes place through their shared belonging within their community of practice in higher education. They define this belonging as being able to negotiate local ways of belonging to the university (the learning environment) and also to broader styles and discourses (society at large) and the Academy, which is distinguished from the university in that the Academy represents a wider notion of knowledge as the structure within which the value of education is globally understood. Asian women constructed their sense of belonging in an ambiguous way: the security of their familiar worlds of like minded women, that is their communities of practice, are at a significant distance from the unfamiliar worlds of white, middle class society and particularly academics.

The shared practices which connect Asian women within higher education are on the one hand clear and precise – they have an ultimate goal which binds them together – but on the other hand, these shared practices are diverse, complex and multi-faceted. The development of a shared repertoire, ways of doing things, such as words and gestures, is something that has been adopted during the course of the existence of the community of practice and becomes part of the practice. The practices they engaged in included discourses by which they could create meanings about their world of higher education as well as the ways in which they expressed their forms of membership and their identities as members.

Identities and diversities

The concept of identity has recently received much attention. The academic literature on identity has focused on the concept of an ethnic identity. It emphasised the complexity of ethnic identity (Back, 1996; Hall, 1990) and explored the interrelationship of diversities such as gender, class, sexuality and religion (Bradley, 1996; Brah, 1996). Hall's work on 'new ethnicities' and the scholarly debate it helped to stimulate has provided new ways of analysing ethnic identities. His premise was based on analysing the complexity of identities and the positions they occupy in modern societies. Hall (1996) argued that identity (and identification) is a never-ending process of construction and reconstruction; it will always continue and one will never reach a final conclusion. The process of identity (and identification) operates across difference and involves the marking out of symbolic boundaries. Hall argued that,

> identities are never unified and in late modern times, increasingly fragmented and fractured; never singular but multiply constructed across different, often intersecting and antagonistic discourses, practices and positions. They are subject to a radical historicization, and are constantly in the process of change and transformation. (1996:17)

In this sense, identity is dynamic, constantly changing and is never static. Further, identity for Hall is linked to notions of power that are the product of difference and exclusion; it is an elusive and constantly changing concept but one that foregrounds understandings of difference, in particular cultural difference and the subjective understandings of that difference. Hall's main argument centres on the premise that identity transcends place, time and history.

Ethnicity and identity

The fluidity of Hall's notion of identity runs counter to influential work by Barth (1969) which argued that it is ethnic boundaries which define a group, and which separate one ethnic group from another. Groups are able to maintain their own identity when members interact with each other. On the one hand, the groups have different criteria for membership; these are based on exclusion and inclusion. If individuals are identified as being from the same ethnic group it suggests that individuals share particular criteria. On the other hand, when strangers who are not members of the ethnic group, are identified, limitations and a lack of shared understandings are recognised. Recognition of who is and who is not a member of a group reinforces boundary maintenance in which cultural differences and cultural boundaries exist. According to Barth (1969), ethnic groups are categories of self-identification and ascription by others. An ethnic group is defined not by its cultural characteristics but by reference to the process of boundary formation. Certain signifiers such as a common history, shared language, customs and traditions may construct ethnic boundaries.

Other researchers have examined the concept of ethnic identity in relation to culture and gender to emphasise the intersectionality of difference (Brah, 1996). Brah's work in particular demonstrates that, historically, identity has not been examined as a multi-faceted and context-specific construct. To understand Asian identity, she argues, it is vital to recognise the diversity and differences within Asian groups, including differences based around religion, caste, class, age and culture. Brah argues that Asians do not automatically transfer their identities from the Indian sub-continent to the UK; rather their identities are translated via cultural, political and economic dimensions. The notion of culture influences how these identities are confirmed or contested.

Brah (1996) introduced the concept of diaspora in order to understand the notion of difference, diversity and identity. She examined this concept from the perspective that different diasporas intersect so it is important to examine how groups are constructed similarly to or differently from each other. The positioning of these groups will also be based on their relationship to the dominant group. Such a concept of diaspora enables us to understand how outsiders are positioned in relation to each other as well as in relation to the dominant groups in society who may be part of the positioning process. Brah states, 'the concept of diaspora signals ... processes of *multi-locationality across geographical, cultural and psychic boundaries*' (1996:194 original emphasis) and goes on to argue that '*Diasporic identities are at once local and global. They are networks of transnational identifications encompassing 'imagined' and 'encountered' communities*' (1996:196 original emphasis). She goes on to examine the concept of 'diaspora space', which she defines as 'the point at which boundaries of inclusion and exclusion, of belonging and otherness, of 'us' and 'them' are contested' (1996:220). Here 'diaspora space' refers to groups who belong within that space as well as those outside it.

Recent research by Parekh (2008:9) has also explored the notion of identity from a multifaceted perspective. He suggests identity has three interrelated dimensions which are inseparable and flow into each other. Firstly he identifies *personal identity* which refers to biographical details and a sense of selfhood or subjectivity; secondly there is *social identity* which refers to how individuals define and distinguish themselves from others, perhaps in terms of their membership of different ethnic, religious and cultural groups; and finally, *individual identity* which refers to how individuals define how they should live their lives and how they conduct themselves as human beings in modern society.

Asian Identity

Concepts used to define those from Asian backgrounds have been contested and debated. Early literature in the 1980s criticised in particular the use of the term 'Black' when it was applied to those from Asian backgrounds. Black was a concept used as a political term to describe non-white groups. Hazareesingh (1986) and Modood (1988) maintained that the term Black referred primarily to the experiences of those of African descent and not to the historical experiences of Asians. They criticised the concept for denying Asian cultural identity, as there are many differences *between* and *within* the diversity of cultural experiences for Asian and African groups. The concept 'Black' is problematic also because many Asians did not identify with it and would not use it to define themselves. Neither would many individuals from African and Caribbean groups define Asian groups as Black. It was argued that the term conceals the cultural differences and needs of groups not of African Caribbean heritage (Brah, 1996).

Alternatives to the concept Black were suggested. Hazareesingh (1986) and Modood (1988) argued that the term Black should be used to refer to those of African Caribbean heritage and Asians should adopt the term 'Indian', since those of Asian origin have a shared historical past. However such a concept fails to examine the origins of those from Bangladeshi and Pakistani backgrounds, who may not want to identify with the concept Indian and whose experiences may be very different. Modood (1988) suggested the term 'Asian' and dismissed the term 'South Asian' as an academic term. Recently, many Asian groups have emphasised the importance of religion in defining their cultural heritage (see Shain, 2003).

Asian women's belongings to communities of practice are based on the notion of boundaries within these groups. The boundaries of membership may be based on ethnicity, religion, gender and age or on being part of a group who share similar cultural and racial experiences. There is a belief that within this membership women share a history and a future and it is from this basis that the boundaries are constructed and membership of the community is formed. The construction of boundaries may shift and women's membership of their communities may also change, depending on where they are at a specific time.

However, as is shown in later chapters, many Asian women of whatever religious or ethnic background define themselves as *British Asian*. They see themselves as being part of both cultures and belonging to both. There is no longer an emphasis on being either just Asian or just British; many younger women have very different experiences to those of their parents. What is more, many are proud to call themselves *British Asian* despite never having visited the Indian sub-continent.

It is important to note that concepts such as Asian culture, arranged marriages, dowries, are constructed around racialised discourses and may be problematic. Such concepts are not necessarily viewed as fixed categories; rather they are constantly changing, fluid and shaped through everyday interactions with the social world. These concepts are interrelated with social divisions such as class, gender, age and generational differences. Such identities are not fixed but are constantly being negotiated.

This chapter has examined the concepts of community and identity, drawing on Wenger's notion of community of practice. It has considered how notions of community have been used to explore how individuals belong or do not belong to particular communities of identity.

3

Race, gender and identity

As a British Indian woman originally from a working class background who has moved into the Academy and is now positioned in many people's eyes as a middle class woman, I was able to identify with my respondents. In many senses I shared the life trajectory of coming from a traditionally understood background of second generation British Asians and also being someone who had been exposed to the possibilities and opportunities to lead a different type of life. I identified with the respondents as well as having shared empathy and understanding. The respondents saw me as one of them – they felt able to open up to me and tell me about their experiences of what it felt like to be an Asian woman and about their experiences of racism in British society. The interview became more like a conversation, a sharing of ideas and views between two people who shared similar experiences.

> I can speak to you and say these things because I know you will understand. You know where I am coming from and you will not think I am saying things that are alien because you have the same experiences of the culture as me and you know about it – which is different for say if a white person was doing the research.

> Being able to speak to you – you are someone from the same sort of background like me and you have probably got a better understanding of our lives and traditions than someone else has – so I can speak to you openly about these experiences and know that you will respect what I am saying and be able to understand.

Many of the women felt a cultural familiarity in the research process. They were comfortable speaking to me about intimate and sensitive issues. Their identification with me enabled them to open up and reveal personal aspects of their lives, which they might otherwise not have had the opportunity to previously discuss.

> Because we have this sort of identity that we share, because you are able to understand things about my life – like my culture – I do feel quite ok speaking to you, I suppose you could say that I feel safe. I feel comfortable because I don't think you're going to laugh at what I'm going to say. You will understand and you will respect what I say and where I'm coming from.

> It's about feeling comfortable with someone, knowing that they understand what you are saying and also knowing that they have also some experience of your sort of culture and the sort of life that you have. Some of the cultural things I know that you will understand because you have probably experienced them yourself, but also I don't think you will think that these experiences are strange or unusual. Some people who don't know much about the culture may think those things and may judge you on that basis. But you will not do that.

This cultural familiarity was emphasised when the respondents used words such as 'us', 'our culture', 'what we do'. They discussed the differences between white and Asian cultures:

> In *our* culture there are things that *we* do that are different to white people. *We're* not the same as them. *Me and you* are different, *we're* Asian and so *we* are able to understand each other (author emphasis).

> *We* have the same sort of culture and *we* have the same sort of experiences that we are able to understand, perhaps other people won't be able to understand those experiences because they have not experienced them, but we have (author emphasis).

Many of the women also spoke about the importance of gender and emphasised that speaking to a woman about their experiences of family and cultural life enabled them to open up and feel comfortable within the interview situation. Early feminist research emphasised the importance of 'woman to woman interviewing' (see Oakley, 1981). Finch (1984) argued that women more than men were used to accepting intrusions into their private lives and observed that the interview conducted in an informal manner by another woman in the setting of the interviewee's own home can take the character of an intimate conversation. Devault (1990) maintained that women interviewing women bring to the interview a tradition of 'woman talk' in which they are able to help each other to develop ideas and so generate discussion around sensitive topics.

Oakley's later research provided a new post-positivist paradigm for the social sciences (Oakley, 2000). Oakley advocated the use of quantitative and experimental methods as 'providing what is often a sounder basis for claiming that we know anything' (2000:14). But, in qualitative research, gender differences between the researcher and the researched can be important in conducting research which revolves around sensitive gendered experiences (Anderson and Umberson, 2004). The gender of the researchers may influence their own perceptions of the experiences of the research participants. Gender can affect how we are seen by our respondents and what they may or may not want to tell us. As indicated below.

> I know that there are things that I am saying to you that I would not say to a man, because they are personal to me and I feel I can trust you. Also speaking to another woman makes me feel more comfortable and more able to speak and open up about things with you.

> There are just some things that you would want to speak to women about, that you know another woman would understand and a man would not. An Asian woman would understand some of the expectations that parents have of us and that we have to be careful how we behave so that we don't give our parents a bad name and all those things. You probably know what I mean when I say that, but I think if you were a man – because men are treated in our culture – you would not be able to understand what I was referring to.

It is this positioning as 'insiders' which enabled Asian women to have a shared empathy with me in my role as the researcher. Ahmad (2003:56) has argued that our positioning as researchers can impact on the kind of research we want to or are allowed to focus on, the support we receive from those in positions of power and the perceptions they have of us and our research. Often if we as black feminists, choose to study subjects that are from our own communities, our work may be dismissed as being 'defensive', 'apologetic' or anecdotal and incidental (Ahmad, 2003). As an Asian woman I had a racialised understanding of my respondents which was emphasised by our sharing of racialised identity and being othered. This heightened the nuanced understanding I felt able to develop by researching people with a similar background to myself. Because of our shared identity, respondents could discuss personal and often intimate details of their lives with me. Race will always affect the research relationship and dictate how we are positioned and how we position ourselves within it. It will influence what respondents tell us and what we tell them. Race infuses all aspects of the research relationship. Within the research, women were not positioned as other; rather they were positioned as women who were part of a group that was similar to my own – together we were othered, together we were outsiders and together we shared our experiences of racism, of constantly being positioned on the margins.

I shared the experience of the silent, unspoken racism we felt we experienced daily, and that was the more troubling because it was hard to pin down or prove existed to someone who did not share such experiences. 'It's when they look at you in that way – you just know, you can't put your finger on it and you can't prove it, but you just know'. This respondent went on to explain, 'It's how they make you feel, it's usually something small like ignoring what you say or making you feel that what you have said has no importance'. I told my respondents about my experiences when working within the Academy: how often I encountered the assumption that I am not an academic but a student or an administrator and the looks of surprise and alarm when my relatively senior academic position becomes apparent. And, perhaps still more troubling, the peers and colleagues who do know my background but who struggle to make eye contact at departmental meetings and who seem content to assume that I will have nothing to contribute to such meetings.

Beyond the Academy, we discussed our experiences of living in multicultural Britain and how racism impacted on us. I discussed with several respondents my experiences of moving from London to a white rural village in which my children's preschool teacher informed me, 'we don't have coloured children here, but we do celebrate events like Diwali and Chinese New Year'. My respondents and I could understand these comments and remarks in a particular way that reflected our shared understanding. We knew how such comments made us feel; we knew we shared a sisterhood, a commonality of being 'outsiders' in a society which still regarded us as 'different' and 'alien'. As articulately expressed here:

> Even though we've been here [in the UK] for years and years and our parents have been here for a long time, people still regard us as being so different to them. They see us as a bit strange because of our customs and so they put us in a box and make judgements about us. But we're not that different to them are we? Some Asian people do exactly what the white and black people do – but others want to keep on to some part of their culture and don't want to entirely be like them [white and black people].

> Sometimes when people look at you and they see that you are not white – you are Asian they make judgements about you. They think that you will have an arranged marriage and they can also make other judgements about you as well – sometimes they will think you can't speak English or they go the other way –

they think you're really rich and privileged. Some people have very negative views of Asian people and some people think we're all rich.

Power and research

Within the research relationship there will always be complex issues of power inequalities between researcher and respondent. It is generally assumed that the basis of power lies with the researcher and not the respondent. But this is not always the case. In many instances it is the respondent who has the power, as they have control over what they are willing to tell us. They can exercise their power by withholding information. Giddens (1985) argues that power will always be part of the research relationship and power is not simply a have/have not aspect of the research process, but that the subjective experience can be complex and indeed ambivalent for the researcher and the researched. Often, though, it is the researcher who is in the position of power; as researchers for example we are writing and theorising about *their* lives in books and articles published within *our* academic world. We are the ones who are in control of the research relationship, we hold the pen and notebook and we determine the interview questions.

In my research relationship with my respondents I sought to minimise power relations between myself and the respondents as far as was possible. By constantly examining and re-examining the development of relationships and the shifts in power relations it is possible to weight power back towards respondents and away from the researcher. One of the ways this was achieved was by revealing personal aspects of my life and enabling the respondents to identify with me and my situation as an Asian woman living in British society. The more I revealed about myself, the more I felt respondents could open up to me. Power relations were thus reduced. Minimising – or trying to minimise – power relationships is based on how we perceive our respondents and how they perceive us. If we are members of the same groups, then there tends to be identification with our respondents and a shared reality reveals a shared empathy and understanding. In my research, many of the women said they felt comfortable speaking to me about their experiences of being 'outsiders' and being 'othered' and they also spoke about their experiences of racism and the impact this had on their lives:

> I think you know what I mean don't you? There are things that I just don't have to explain to you that you will just understand. You are an Asian woman and you know the things that I am speaking about. When I tell you that people have called me names because I am Asian, I think you will know what I mean – haven't we all experienced people calling us names because we are Asian?

You can only speak to someone who has experienced something for them to fully understand it. You have experienced what it's like for someone to say something to you or treat you in a certain way because of the colour of your skin or because of where you come from. So you are able to understand this. Someone who hasn't experienced this could not understand it in the same way. You have to be careful who you tell, some people who have not had that experience may think you are the one with the problem because you are over dramatising it or over analysing.

The research relationship is fluid and dynamic and constantly changing during the course of any research. Researchers do not always hold the power or have *complete* control over the research relationship throughout the project. I wanted the women to have the opportunity to tell their stories about their lives and to feel comfortable and able to do so without feeling in any way threatened. I agree with Campbell and Wasco (2000:787) that the ultimate goal of feminist research is to 'identify the ways in which multiple forms of oppression impact women's lives and empower women to tell their stories by providing a respectful and egalitarian research environment'.

I sought to use Renzetti's advice (1997:134) that 'researchers are encouraged to start from their own experience, to freely share information about themselves, their personal lives, and their opinions with those they are studying; and adhere to a feminist ethic of care'. A feminist methodology thus commits to giving voice to the personal everyday experiences of women, particularly the women who continue to be marginalised in society. As researchers we are not separate from our own experiences and backgrounds. So we have to be critically aware of our self in the research process and the influence our lived experience and knowledge has on the research. Self-reflexivity is an important tool which requires us to be aware of the self in the research process, particularly in the creating of knowledge.

Different voices will emerge within the research process and the research relationship. I sought to be sensitive to the needs of my research respondents, an important factor when conducting research with those who are marginalised and 'othered' (Jewekes *et al*, 2005). Asian women for example may feel they have traditionally been silenced and disempowered. Reinharz and Chase (2002:225) contend that as feminist researchers who interview women we need to be aware and understand the impact that research involvement may have on women: 'She may discover her thoughts, learn who she is and find her voice'. This was emphasised by several of the respondents:

I have found it interesting speaking to you. In a way I have kind of found it to be therapeutic – it has made me think of things more clearly. It is because I have been telling you about these things – like it makes me realise who I am and appreciate my culture more, because it is part of who I am.

I have enjoyed having our conversations because it has been interesting to know what you think, why you are doing this research and why you think it is all important. I also think that it has made me more aware of how my own experience as an Asian woman is a big part of coming to university. It's also good for us to be able to talk about our lives and to get rid of some of the stereotypes that people have of us. They think we are all the same and judge us from that basis. Many people make their judgements by what they see on the TV and hear on the news – and we know those are stereotypes.

In conducting research with groups who are othered, self-disclosure is important. It encourages the participants to elaborate on their personal and subjective experiences. If researchers are willing to share with respondents their own personal experiences, this will encourage respondents to open up. Reinharz and Chase (2002:227) suggest that researchers' self-disclosure occurs when the researcher 'shares ideas, attitudes and/or experiences concerning matters that might relate to the interview topic in order to encourage respondents to be more forthcoming'. This is part of the process in which the researcher can think about their own social location in the research process.

This chapter has examined the position of Asian women in society. It has explored the use of Black feminist methodology in conducting the research and has argued that by engaging in research with minority ethnic women, Black feminist methodology is a useful standpoint from which to conduct the research. It is a positive means by which we as Black, Asian, othered researchers who sit outside the confines of the privileged white, middle class academy are able to understand the experiences of women who are themselves othered.

These women's lives are also positioned within a specific set of circumstances that sit outside of the dominant society. A Black feminist standpoint provides us with ways of engaging with minority ethnic women in a positive and empathic way in which shared experience reveals shared empathy and shared understanding. Such a sharing of experiences can encourage women to speak about their own experiences, without feeling they will be silenced. In the need to share experiences about our lives between an Asian woman researcher and Asian women university students there is also a hint of the collaborative practices that can make it easier for outsiders to work within different institutions. If the Academy has not been the traditional preserve of

Asian women and still represents itself as an institution which is more comfortable with white male students, I sought in my research to understand the processes that were used by a group of outsiders to ease their passage across alien terrain.

4

Asian women's experiences
in higher education

The picture that has emerged of ethnic minority groups' engagement with higher education in the last 15 years is generally unclear. Not only have there been dramatic shifts in the numbers of students attending university in the UK, there have also been significant structural changes to the university system. Patterns of migration to the UK have fluctuated and changed. The process of collating meaningful data and analysing it to establish generalisable trends has often proved difficult for researchers. There is also a real fear that much work simply arrives too late; that by the time a project has completed and papers finally published, the world has moved on and institutions are faced with new challenges. So whilst it is often relatively straightforward to make broad-brush pronouncements such as providing evidence that some minority ethnic groups are overrepresented in higher education whilst others are underrepresented, this often fails to highlight other important issues. Much of the research on Asian women in higher education has ignored differences between and within the different Asian groups (Connor *et al*, 2004) and relied on small scale samples (Ahmad *et al*, 2003), as we have seen.

Research using official statistics has shown differences in participation between ethnic groups based on subject and choice of institution. Shiner and Modood (2002) demonstrate that university applicants from ethnic minorities tend to receive places at 'new' universities (former polytechnics) rather than the older ones. What is more, graduates from old universities are more likely to be recruited by prestigious and higher paying firms than those from new universities, thus furthering a 'cumulative pattern of ethnic disadvantage' (2002:228). Parents' social class and educational background influences the educational success of their children in which middle class parents use their knowledge to fund the right kind of institution – the one which offers the best course for their children. Reay *et al* (2005:vii) argue that the choice of higher education institutions plays a significant part in reconstituting and reproducing the divisions and hierarchies that exist in higher education and perpetuating the advantage of those from middle class backgrounds over those from working class backgrounds.

Modood (2006) has argued that students from minority ethnic groups are not only likely to attend less prestigious universities, but are also more likely to drop out before completing their degree and, with the exception of Indian and Chinese students, are less likely to obtain a high grade on completion. There are differences in achievement and attendance at higher education for groups which fall under the category South Asian: those of Indian back-grounds are more likely to be educated to degree level than those of Pakistani and, last of all, Bangladeshi backgrounds (ONS Social Trends No. 36). Social class, religion, culture and the effect of schools all have an impact on the per-formance and success in higher education of minority ethnic groups (Abbas, 2004) and their representation between universities, subjects, regions and courses varies accordingly (Connor *et al*, 2004).

The last decade has seen increasing participation in higher education for all minority ethnic groups suggesting they have benefited by its expansion since the 1990s. Minority ethnic groups are more likely than white British groups to continue to stay in education after completing compulsory schooling. How-ever, some groups are still more likely than their white British peers to have no qualifications: 47 per cent of Bangladeshis and 41 per cent of Pakistanis have no qualifications compared to a figure of 30 per cent amongst the White British population (ONS Social Trends, No. 36).

More generally, minority ethnic students are more likely to attend universities in which there are high numbers of minority ethnic students already attend-ing. According to Reay *et al* (2005), 'Institutions which offer an ethnic mix, with good numbers of the student's own ethnicity but no predominant group, are favoured' (114).

Many students choose to attend universities serving their local and geo-graphical communities. For many Asian students, leaving home is rarely an option. Whilst this may reflect parental pressure it also reflects the impor-tance attached to family commitments and relationships, which are valued highly (Reay *et al*, 2005). Ironically, despite family pressures which may res-trict students' choice of institution, the family plays a bigger part in encouraging their young people to participate in higher education than do white working class families (Connor *et al*, 2004). Education has been used by minority ethnic groups to further social mobility and is one of the reasons why families place a high value on success in higher education (Modood *et al*, 1997).

The socio-demographic profile of minority ethnic groups in the UK

The minority ethnic population has grown rapidly in the UK since the 1950s. It was about 1 million in 1967, 3.1 million in 1991 and 4.6 million in 2001 (Green *et al*, 2005), growing from 5.6 per cent of the population in 1991 to 8 per cent in 2001. This includes individuals from a diverse range of backgrounds, including Indian, Pakistani and Bangladeshi, Chinese, mixed heritage and African and Caribbean. Of the 7.9 per cent who make up the total minority ethnic population Indians are the largest group (1.8%), followed by Pakistani (1.3%) and Bangladeshi (0.5%). Black Caribbean's constitute 1 per cent and Black African 0.8 per cent. Chinese groups constitute 0.4 per cent (ONS Social Trends, No. 36).

Compared to white Britons, the majority of minority ethnic groups have younger populations. For example, compared to 22 per cent of white women, 29 per cent of Indian women, 44 per cent of Pakistani women and 47 per cent of Bangladeshi women are under the age of 20 (Hudson and Sahin-Dikmen, 2007). This young profile suggests that the proportion of minority ethnic women in the working population will increase rapidly over future decades (Strategy Unit, 2003).

The diversity of Asian women's experiences in higher education

Asian women can be regarded as a distinct cohort of students with some similarity of background but also as a group of distinct and different students whose backgrounds distinguish them from each other. Some of the stereotypical interpretations that persist around British Asians and particularly Asian women cause some confusion over the similarities and differences and the impact these may have. So for example, representations of Asian women in universities as unassuming and quiet, culturally shackled to patriarchal structures in the home and likely at any moment to be flown 'back home' for an arranged marriage are misplaced, but they nevertheless feature in the popular media and this itself has an impact on how Asian women feel about themselves.

Ethnicity does play a key role in defining some trends amongst students. Students from minority ethnic backgrounds have, on average, lower entry qualifications reflecting the less traditional routes many take to university. Fewer take the conventional A- level route and Pakistani and Bangladeshi students in particular are more likely than their white, Indian or Chinese peers to come to higher education via further education colleges (Connor *et al*, 2004). Some of these differences are also reflected in student attainment. Far fewer Bangladeshis (14%) or Pakistanis (18%) living in the UK are educated to degree level than the Chinese (37%) or Indian (31%) population (Simpson *et al*, 2006). These figures can be compared to that of the white British population of 18 per cent being educated to degree level, suggesting that some parts of British Asian society are embracing higher education to a greater degree than the population overall.

Muslim women's experiences in higher education have been particularly well documented. Much evidence points to their high level of participation but at the same time, many questions have been raised about their experience of education. There is for example clear evidence that Muslim women are more likely to attend new post-1992 universities, the former polytechnics (Archer and Leathwood, 2003), and this may have a negative impact on their future careers. That said, Tyrer and Ahmad (2005) discuss how Muslim women's identity changes in relation to their continuing engagement with higher education, noting how those of the second and third generation value it for its influence on their careers and life chances. Bagguley and Hussain (2007) found that the number of Bangladeshi and Pakistani women participating in higher education has risen, that they have high job aspirations and that they had received strong parental support for their decision. The authors report that 'although women of Pakistani and Bangladeshi origin have been one of the fastest rates of increase in participation in higher education, they still remain among the most excluded groups from university education' (2007:1). This exclusion is based on their participation in higher education compared to other Asian groups, such as those from Indian backgrounds.

Muslim women and their identities are particularly likely to be understood in light of stereotypical assumptions about their lives and a perceived problematic relationship with British society, so many find themselves perceived by other students, administrators and teaching staff at the university as suffering from a 'culture clash' (Coleman, 2005; Malik, 2005). Their experiences fall within an essentialist perspective that fails to attribute to Muslim women students anything like as great a degree of agency to that of other students.

Despite popular perceptions however, Muslim women's choices are not limited because of their cultural and religious backgrounds (Tyrer and Ahmad,

2005). Their experiences are located within the production and reproduction of gender and racialised discourses of Muslim identities (Archer, 2002). Like all students, they are using their time at university to develop and strengthen aspects of their identity.

Research shows that Muslim students are more likely to experience racism in higher education than other minority ethnic students. The Federation of Student Islamic Societies (2005) found that over 75 per cent of Muslim students (from a sample of 401 students) had experienced verbal religious abuse. Bagguley and Hussain (2007) found that the Bangladeshi and Pakistani women in their study experienced racism from both university staff and students. These researchers found that when that when they asked Careers Officers about the support they offered to Asian women, the replies emphasised that concerns around marriage and parental preference for subjects and careers such as Medicine and Law influenced the advice they gave them. They said that such career choices were sometimes unrealistic and reflected family expectations. Some careers officers suggested that Asian women might be entering higher education as a strategy for postponing getting married.

The labour market

The labour market profile of minority ethnic groups is well documented. Research shows that over the last decades the overall position of disadvantage has turned into one of differential achievements both between and within minority ethnic groups. There is not only an employment gap between groups but also difference in terms of participation in the labour market and unemployment rates (Simpson *et al*, 2006).

A direct link has been found in performance in higher education and success in the labour market. Those from minority ethnic backgrounds have greater difficulty finding the jobs and careers they want, so are more likely to turn to further education or training after their degrees (Connor *et al*, 2004). Bangladeshi and Pakistani women are more likely than Indian or white women to be economically inactive. The low economic activity rates of older Pakistani and Bangladeshi women are given much attention and have been attributed to multiple barriers to employment, such as poor English language skills and lack of qualifications, and also cultural and religious preferences to do with family life and paid employment (Dale *et al*, 2002). Dale *et al* (2002) found that expectations and aspirations of younger Pakistani and Bangladeshi women have changed, the higher labour market participation rates for those under 24 seem to confirm this trend.

Ahmad *et al* (2003) argue that Asian women born and brought up in the UK have a very different profile from their mothers: they are highly educated, ambitious and keen to progress up the career ladder. Simpson *et al* (2006) examined the importance of qualifications for participation in the labour market and they argue that qualifications are important in explaining the different rates of economic activity for different ethnic groups. They found, that amongst female graduates born in the UK, economic activity rates exceed 70 per cent for Bangladeshi and Pakistani women. Another useful indicator of labour market performance is the employment rate. Among women aged 25 and over, Bangladeshi (16%) and Pakistani (23%) women are the least likely to be in paid employment compared to Indian (63%), white British and Caribbean women (70%) (Simpson *et al*, 2006). The employment performance of most minority ethnic groups improved between 1991 and 2001 (Clark and Drinkwater, 2007).

For women aged 25 and over, Bangladeshi (16%) and Pakistani (23%) women are least likely to be in paid employment and white British (71%), Caribbean (70%) and Indian women (62%) are the most likely (Simpson *et al*, 2006). Unemployment rates for Bangladeshi, Pakistani and African women range between 12 and 16 per cent, compared to the national average of 5 per cent and are 4-5 times more likely to be unemployed than white British women. Indian women also show low levels of unemployment (5.8%) (Simpson *et al*, 2006). Factors relating to unemployment have been identified as being linked to such issues as language skills, differences in educational qualifications and length of stay in the UK. Berthoud (2000) describes these factors as the 'ethnic penalty' that reflects the discrimination in the labour market. There are no language barriers for British born individuals from minority ethnic groups yet there is evidence that they do not have the same opportunities in the labour market as their white counterparts, even though they have invested in similar routes such as higher education (Carmichael and Woods, 2000). Despite three decades of anti-discrimination legislation in the UK, women and members of minority ethnic groups continue to be under-represented in professional and senior management positions.

Much of the research demonstrates the disadvantages women from minority ethnic backgrounds face in higher education. However, my study examines how Asian women are using strategies for success in higher education. It explores the choices women make in choosing where to study, which courses they select and the impact this has on their participation in their community of practice in higher education. It also examines the changing dynamic process of identity formation as women move through a transitional period in their lives towards a changing environment in which they have greater control over their lives despite the disadvantages they face in higher education.

Which university?

Many of the women in my study had opted for their nearest, local university or one that was easily commutable from their parental home. There was a direct correlation between their choice of university and their decision to remain at home for the duration of their studies. Although remaining in the family home limited their potential choice of institution, there were also positive reasons for the choice they made. The women thought they would feel more accepted in their local university by other students, as the ethnic mix reflected their home locality: these universities were seen to have a 'critical mass' of similar students. In other words they anticipated finding themselves in a known and comfortable environment. They also said they wanted to avoid having to travel long distances.

> I decided to choose this university because it was my local university, it's near where I live and I also know that the sort of people that go to the university are like me. There are what you call mature students there, people who have done access courses and also other Asian and Black people. It's easy for me to get to and it's easy for me to get to work as well. It's also more likely that I could know the people here and they probably live in the same areas to me or are quite close.

Another respondent welcomed the 'localness' of the university.

> Being local makes a big difference to me, it means that the people at the university are the same as me in some ways, there are probably more Asian and black people who go to the university as well. That makes me feel more comfortable because I think I will fit in with them. I can still keep working because I work locally so won't have to travel long distances to go to the university or to go to work.

This localism enabled women to continue working in paid employment or their children to attend the nurseries and schools they were already registered with. This minimised the disruption for the women and their families.

> My children's nursery is local and near where I live and because the university is a bus ride away, I don't have to change the nursery or change anything else in my life. I can just carry on as I am. When people have to leave home to travel to a new place then that is much harder for them because they have to move and go to a new town and meet new people. Here I will meet new people but

won't have the added burden of moving to a new place and my children won't be disrupted. For me, it's not that much change, you could say it was like going to work and not going to university when you have to move out which is a whole new change to your life.

I work locally, which means I can go to the university, finish there and then go straight to work and know I won't be late. That way I am able to combine the two together and it makes it easier for me to do both. If I went to a university that was far away that would make it harder to combine the working and the studying. I have had this part-time job for a while now, the people know me and so it makes sense to me to stay where I am. Living at home makes sense to me as well, it means I can attend university but I don't have to move out and have such a big change in my life. Living at home means I can do most of the things that other students do – though not all – but that would be the same for anyone who is living at home. It's also cheaper for me to live at home and I like the idea that I can come home to my family and don't have to worry that I may be on my own. They are there to provide me with the different kinds of things that I need.

Attending their local university enabled the women to combine paid work and university. Many valued the convenience: they could study in the library and did not have to spend valuable time commuting. These quotes reflect the importance the women attributed to retaining a certain stability around attending university that contrasted with more traditional ideas of university attendance being an opportunity to be independent. In part, this reflected the backgrounds of the slightly older respondents but primarily it was due to attachment to family structures. The choice of entering higher education was made in parallel to other commitments and responsibilities, such as being a family member or continuing with part-time work. The women valued the proximity of the university for making it easier to maintain these sorts of commitments. They raised this again in discussions about what sort of insti-tutions were suitable for Asian women. Many did not consider applying to a traditional redbrick university, believing they would not fit in or have the academic ability required.

I didn't even consider going to somewhere like Bristol or even LSE because I don't think I would fit in. I wanted to stay local anyway. But for me, I have been through an Access course and I didn't leave school with 3 A-levels so I don't think I would feel right going there. The people that go to those universities are those people who are really bright and are the ones who have backgrounds where they are used to going to those universities. They are the traditional ones where people leave home and go to. They are also different to the old polys.

> These kind of universities like [name of university] accept all sorts of different people and I think that's what makes them more interesting and less threatening than the more traditional ones.

Women spoke about the differences in traditional redbrick universities and the new universities (former polytechnics). They spoke of a divide between the two types of universities which was associated with the types of people who attended. Although many of the women said they were achieving high grades in their assignments and wanted to get first class degrees, they still did not feel they were good enough to attend the more traditional, redbrick universities.

> Even if I did get a first at the end, I don't think even then I would be able to go to a proper university if I wanted to do a masters or something. I think I would feel a bit scared, almost like I shouldn't be there. I would like to carry on after this degree, but I would either stay here or go to another local university. It would depend on the course that I wanted to do. But I wouldn't change from coming here to going to somewhere like the LSE or Kings College. It would be a too big a jump. You have to start at those type of universities to continue there.

What respondents seemed to emphasise above all was the distance they felt existed between who they were and the world they inhabited, and the world of established universities. The desire to attend an institution that was 'like college' reflects a desire not to engage with major change. Asian women were constructing an account of the stability and stasis they could retain in their lives by remaining within their families, continuing with their current commitments and attending a university that was not too different from school or college. To move beyond the local world was associated with instability and the unknown. 'A sense of belonging' was a fundamental requirement for signing up to any institution.

> I feel ok coming here because I think there are lots of other women who are here that are like me. That makes me feel secure because I can identify with them and I can say they don't make me feel like I shouldn't be here, because they feel the same as me. They may be women who left school, maybe got married and had a job and wanted to come back to education. But even the ones who haven't done this – the younger ones – are from the same sort of background as me. They are the sort of people that you can identify with and feel comfortable talking to.

When asked what advice they would give to others about the type of university to attend, many of the women again said that they would emphasise the need to feel secure and have a sense of belonging to the institution.

> I think I would tell friends to go where they felt they would be happy. It also depends where you live. If they went tot their local university, they would feel comfortable there because there would be people like them who go there. If it's an area like this then that would mean there will be quite a lot of Asian and Black people who go to that university and it will be probably more mixed than say a university like Bristol which tends to be more traditional and white.

Attending their local university was a much more secure path into higher education than they felt would be the case if they attended university further afield. Respondents felt that by remaining within their local boundaries they would identify with other women who were like them: women who had taken similar non-traditional routes into university, women who might have children and work part-time and most crucially for all of them, women with an Asian background who shared their understanding of family lives and pressures. This identification with other similar women was crucial for Asian women to enable them to benefit from their experiences in higher education. Being in the university environment provided the basis for bringing like-minded Asian women together, who could share difficulties and strategies for making their lives more comfortable. The communities the women were used to engaging with in their daily lives were in some degree mirrored by the circumstances of the university and it was this coming together of particular sets of similar Asian women that allowed them to recreate communities of practice that would make university life easier.

Which course?

Many of the women had decided to take humanities and social sciences degrees. They saw these areas as attractive fields of study where they could learn about topics which had links to future careers in research, social work, educational psychology, teaching and management. Links towards postgraduate options such as masters' courses were clearly signposted and this offered a clear career focus. Such courses were attractive, as their flexibility enabled the women to focus on areas which interested them.

> I think this kind of degree is good because it would enable me to get into lots of different kinds of jobs like management or even social work. It gives you a wide variety and then later on you can do the things that interest you. I think it aims to provide you with some kind of training that you can take away with you. That is also another difference I think about doing a degree in this kind of university you can get some training. The older, more traditional universities don't always offer you that.

The courses offered women diversity and richness as well as a vocational element which promised success in the labour market. When discussing career advice and future employment choices, many of the women said they found the advice offered by the university careers service useful.

> I have used the careers service here. I have used it twice and it has been very helpful. They help you to think about what you can do with your degree and whether you can get a good job with it or if you need further qualifications or training. I have never found them to be judgemental in any way or make any assumptions about my life. They are just there to help you and that's what they do.

> We do have a careers service here and you can go in and get leaflets and information. You can also make an appointment to see someone if you want to. I have done that because I wasn't sure what it was that I wanted to do and I have to say it was very helpful. The woman I spoke to seemed to have a lot of experience and asked me the right sort of questions so that she could help me. I would say she was very helpful. She also gave me her email and number so that I can call her if I need to speak to her again. I could also make another appointment if I need to. The only issue I would say about the careers service is that they are not open all the time, they are only open certain times. But they are helpful and you can email them and set up an appointment to see someone which a lot of us have done.

Many of the women selected their courses for the variety of knowledge offered and the choices of areas which would provide them with a foundation for future careers. They did not report finding the expectations of careers service and advice personnel stereotypical concerning marriage, as Bagguley and Hussain (2007) reported, but said these services were useful, informative and supportive.

Future careers

Many of the respondents wanted to use their educational qualifications to enter the labour market, be successful in their careers and achieve social mobility. Education was a means of achieving social mobility. They saw their participation in higher education as a route to higher levels in the labour market, but they also said they were looking for something less tangible related to their personal development.

> If you start off with a degree it makes a difference because then you can get a job that is of a much higher level than other people who don't have a degree. It also means that you can study as well – you can study while you are working so all of the time you are improving yourself.

Many felt that getting a degree was their chance of 'improving themselves' and being successful in a competitive labour market. What was interesting about respondents suggesting they had wider, personal goals associated with their degree course was that in many ways this counteracted the slightly weak approach to choosing an institution. So whilst many of the women sought what could be described as an 'easy' option of enrolling in a local university and living in the comfortable surroundings of their parental home rather than rushing headlong towards the independence of student life away from home. Once enrolled on a degree course they still looked towards a much wider set of goals. Their identities were obviously going to be shaped by their experiences of university, but there was a clear sense of this being pushed a bit further by the desire to explore new opportunities, and these would be opportunities that were not available in the domestic environment but were associated with being a student. Unsurprisingly, despite the awareness and interest in personal development, finding a job remained the greatest motivation when considering university.

> These days it's very hard to get a job. It's hard to get a good job that you really want because you know there are so many different people who are applying for one job. So you do have to shine in a way and do better because you want that job – otherwise you won't get anywhere. There are lots of graduates who are unemployed and that's another reason why people do decide to go on and get a Masters because they may not get the job that they want or they may not get a job at all.

Many of the women felt that an increase in competition in the labour market would exacerbate discriminatory practices in employment, but they were still adamant about wanting to succeed. They were aware of the competitive nature of the labour market, but this did not deter them from wanting to enter it. Rather, it made them want to achieve more highly, as they felt they would have to prove themselves to potential employers. In looking towards future careers, women expressed something of their hopes and aspirations and it was hard not to conclude that being at university allowed them some space for self-reflection. Most of the respondents were, if not the first family member, generally amongst the first generation of their families to attend university. Often they talked about the differences between their lives and those of their parents and grandparents. Going to university itself reflected a change in their lives from what might have been anticipated only a few years earlier, but allied with this were changes to do with their potential, including their future jobs and how higher education would affect their changing identities. The university was a site in which Asian women could to some degree scrutinise their identity and renegotiate it.

A changing identity?

I asked the women whether they felt their identities were changing as a result of attending university. Most did not say their identities changed specifically in relation to being at university. Rather, they said, attending university had made them more ambitious and focused about the choices they would have after they left university.

> I don't think coming to university has changed me because I am still the same person. I will always be who I am and I am proud of that. The only way I have changed is that doing this course has made me more ambitious and made me think that, yes I can do it, I can get a degree and do well.

Some women, however were explicit about their identities changing as a result of attending university,

> I guess in some respects you do change when you go to university because you become privileged to some degree, because you can tell people that you have got a degree. When you have finished your degree you have shown that you have achieved a certain way of thinking and a certain way of looking at things without just accepting them.

Some women described how their family members and friends remarked on how they had changed.

> My family think I have changed and they think that I will change when I finish the degree. To be honest I don't think I have changed much. My sister tells me that I am a bit snobby because I read a proper newspaper now. I didn't used to read or buy the paper, but I like reading it, there's lots of interesting articles to read and lot of them are related to things that we are studying. I think that because maybe my sister didn't go to university she feels that I will be a changed person. I will because I want to do more with my life like get a good job and maybe do more studying, but she did not have that opportunity.

This respondent felt she would probably change because this was inevitable, but she did not think she would forget who she was. In many ways, what women described was the process of becoming more self-reflexive and of paying closer attention to what shaped their identity, what facets of their character remain important and where their loyalties lie.

> How could I forget who I am? I will always be me, it's because I am the first person in my family who is going to university so I think they think this will affect

me. It will affect me but I will always be the same person, won't I? I think it will affect my family as well because my younger siblings will want to go to university and they will be encouraged to do so not just by my parents but also from me because I would have had the experience and could help them. There's different sorts of change. There's the change which is inevitable when you go into education. You feel you have more choices and you feel you can do more with your life. But at the end of the day, deep down you are always the same person.

Other respondents who felt that change was inevitable also looked towards their future selves and the impact going to university would have on the type of people they would *become*. Changing was related to 'bettering yourself' and for some women this was also related to how their achievement at university would affect their attitudes towards their own children. Many were positive that their participation in higher education would influence how their own children would see them and many saw themselves as being role models for their children.

This chapter has examined the ways in which Asian women are using strategies for success in higher education. They selected a university in which they would feel comfortable and able to identify with other students who were from similar ethnic backgrounds and shared similar cultural experiences. The women gained support through their networks of support within their communities of practice in higher education. Decisions about degree choice were influenced by flexibility of degree which would lead to a variety of career options that would not restrict them in the labour market or further study. Many of the women spoke about the positive advice they received from the careers service which, they felt, did not restrict them in any way or have particular expectations about Asian women. They also spoke about their changing identities whilst at university. Change was an inevitable part of women's lives but women wanted to use this change in a positive way to achieve social mobility and greater success in the labour market.

5

The Academy

Non-traditional students

An emphasis on making higher education accessible to students who have never traditionally considered it an option has been high on New Labour's educational policy agenda. The Government's White Paper, *The Future of Higher Education,* made a clear commitment to widen participation in higher education. However, despite such policy initiatives, there continues to be unequal access to higher education. There has been concern that non-traditional students such as mature women, those from lower socioeconomic classes and some minority ethnic backgrounds continue to be disadvantaged. As Read *et al* (2003:271-272) point out:

> Academic culture both reflects and reinforces the dominant discourse of the student as white, middle class and male. Becoming comfortable with the culture of academia – and therefore with the university itself – can be slightly more difficult for those who do not fit neatly into these categories.

Recent data has shown that young people in manual social classes remain under-represented in higher education in Britain. Despite increasing from a participation rate of 11 per cent in 1991/92 to 19 per cent in 2001/02, participation remains well below that of the non-manual social classes, where participation rates have increased from 35 per cent to 50 per cent over the same period. The percentage of students from minority ethnic groups accepted to higher education institutions through the Universities and Colleges Admissions Service (UCAS) has also increased. Students of Indian origin continued to make up the largest proportion of non-white undergraduates: 4.2 per cent of all undergraduates in 2002/03 compared with 3.8 per cent in 1990/91 and 4.8 per cent in 2001/02. Students of Black African origin, however, have seen the largest increase since 1990/91, up from 0.7 per cent to 1.9 per cent (ONS Social Trends, 24) .

This chapter begins with a brief overview of the problems facing non-traditional students and their experiences in higher education before considering how these can be challenged by the students.

The culture of higher education

Despite the rise in the numbers of students from working class and minority ethnic backgrounds attending university, the culture of the university and the academy remains white, middle class and male (Bhopal, 2008; Grant, 1997). Consequently, students from non-traditional backgrounds are placed as 'outsiders' within higher education and so are disadvantaged by the culture of the university (Bhopal, 2008; Tett, 2000). This culture is based on middle class values which affect the ways in which students think, write and behave in higher education (Lea and Street, 2000). For instance it influences the choices non-traditional students make when deciding which universities to attend (Bhopal, 2008; Reay et al, 2001). Often choice of institution is reflected in the extent to which students feel they will fit in with the institution, especially for those from working class and minority ethnic backgrounds who may feel their choices are limited (Reay et al, 2001).

Being an 'outsider' or feeling like an outsider will also affect the experience of being at university. Some students may feel they are entering unknown territory; if they are the first person in their family to attend university they may have little idea what to expect. Just attending an institution might be an uncomfortable experience. If they feel they do not fit in with the expectations of the university or with its social and ethnic mix, they may struggle to engage in all aspects of university life.

Choice and type of institution

The idea of mass higher education, rather than decreasing societal division has actually contributed to a more divided and elitist system of higher education in which those from non-traditional backgrounds such as mature students, minority ethnic groups and working class students are arguably disadvantaged even further (Hutchings and Archer, 2001). With the divide between old universities and new, it is apparent that students attending the old universities tend to attain higher paid jobs and more successful careers. For many non-traditional students the desire to attend universities where they feel they will belong (Reay et al, 2001) or where they feel they can identify with other students, particularly when that identification is made on the basis of ethnicity (Bhopal, 2008; 2009), tends to push them towards their local new university. Reay *et al* (2001) identify a hierarchy of status attributed to universities which is well understood by school leavers. They report that students from non-traditional backgrounds are neither prompted to apply to more prestigious institutions by school careers advisors for example, nor do they feel they are likely to be accepted by them. This is in stark contrast to public school educated, white middle class pupils who are likely to be prompted by careers advisors to apply to the old universities, where it is assumed they will feel comfortable. The cumulative effect of concerns about the culture of potential institutions, the pressures to remain local and near the family home and the lack of professional encouragement to attend an old university channel many non-traditional students, including Asian women, towards new universities.

Socio-economic class

A continuing government concern has been the under-representation of students from lower socio economic groups in higher education (Robertson and Hillman, 1997). Although the number of working class students attending universities has increased, it is the number of middle class students which has risen dramatically (Davies, 1995), with the result that inequality between classes in relation to higher education remains constant and is unlikely to change soon (Hatcher, 1998). Social class continues to be a powerful predictor of educational attainment, with fewer young people from lower socio-economic classes achieving the minimum entry requirements for higher education (Bynner *et al*, 1997).

There are ongoing concerns that middle class children are better equipped to make choices about higher education, largely because university education is part of the structure that divides society along class lines. Parents and children from working class backgrounds are more likely to perceive higher education as a culture dominated by the middle classes and one in which they will feel alienated (Lynch and O'Riordan, 1998). Middle class parents are likely to know more about higher education and its processes than working class parents so are better positioned to advise their children about the courses and types of institutions they should attend (Reay, 1998).

Ethnicity

Ethnic differences also affect achievement in higher education. Modood and Shiner (1994) argued that pre-1992 universities are less likely to accept applicants from minority ethnic groups and lower socio-economic groups even when their qualifications are the same as those from middle class backgrounds. Moreover, financial constraints drive more students from working class and minority ethnic backgrounds to attend their local university (see chapter 6). Research by Cheng and Heath (1993) examined the complex patterns which exist in the relationship between education, class and race and how different patterns based on different family backgrounds, emerge. Their analysis confirms both the demographic in the new universities and the variation in participation of minority ethnic groups in higher education (Coffield and Vignoles, 1997).

Mature women students

As their participation in higher education has increased from the 1970s onwards, the educational experience of mature students has become a focus of analysis. Many mature students have children of their own and other family commitments to consider when attending university. In particular, female mature students are seen as posing problems for higher education which tends to be geared towards students without family responsibilities (Edwards, 1993). Universities are less likely than many workplaces to be geared towards providing childcare facilities and flexible timetables (Britton and Baxter, 1999). Edwards (1993) argues that the university is constructed around a male model that denies the specificity of female experience and the ways in which gender constructs the experience of education. For some women the structure of much university life sits almost in diametric opposition to their daily lives: household management tasks such as getting children ready for school, shopping, and preparing meals, will inevitably clash with traditional university timetables. So a single parent who bears the responsibility of raising children has little choice other than the nearest university.

Hutchings and Archer (2001) note how having a positive identification to their local area influences the choice of university of men from African Caribbean backgrounds. It is often a successful strategy because it takes account of factors that make university attendance feel more comfortable for students whose family do not have a background of higher education. By attending their local university such students rightly anticipate they will be surrounded by people of similar backgrounds and by other groups who are familiar because they live in the same area. This gives students a sense of security and belonging (Bhopal, 2008), since their knowledge of their locality is transferable to the university setting. Although they may be entering an institution in which the academic structures are an unknown quantity they are doing so amongst peers who share similar social values and who are equally uncomfortable with their new surroundings.

Despite these recognised difficulties, non-traditional students continue to challenge the dominant culture of the university, they also adapt in order to be successful (Read *et al*, 2003). Mirza (1992) observed that African Caribbean women are prepared to sacrifice immediate pleasures for long-term gain. Issues of upward mobility and sacrifice are therefore important. Mirza (1997) also points to the high aspirations of women from African Caribbean backgrounds for upward class mobility and success in higher education as one means of achieving them. Many African Caribbean women faced severe challenges, yet continued to strive for success in education.

Hutchings and Archer (2001:88) found that many children from minority ethnic backgrounds came from families which had a tradition of 'bettering themselves': They identified the long-term benefits of attending university and encouraged their children to attend university. Such families were looking to greater social mobility for both their children and the whole family.

One of the challenges for Asian women is to attend a university in which they feel they will not stand out and where they will find a shared identity and a sense of belonging with students from similar backgrounds. Other advantages include being able to continue living at home and not having to face the challenge of financial debt. Localism enabled women to feel confident about attending university and enabled their families to give them support. Getting a degree was important to them and they were willing to make personal sacrifices, such as delaying entering the labour market. The following sections examine some of these issues.

Women's identities in the academy

Many of the women spoke about their multi-faceted identity at university through their relationship with the academy – specifically their lecturers. In particular, they described creating a particular kind of identity to counter the way they were seen by the academic staff. Neither the image of themselves they projected nor the image their lecturers held about Asian women matched how they or their families saw themselves.

> Well I think they [lecturers] see us as different anyway, don't they? With them I have to be a professional student because I know they have a great deal of power. They are the ones who are marking my work and ultimately they are the ones who decide what grades I get. So I am a student to them. I would not speak to them about my life at home because I don't think they would understand.

Some of the women spoke of the distance between themselves and their lecturers, which was based on their professional role as students and based also on their 'difference'.

> Some of the other girls do say that they think a few of the lecturers might have certain views of men and women and certain views of Asian women. I think that is inevitable because we all have certain views about groups of people in society. But they are different to us because they are the ones who are teaching us and we are the learners.

These women presented a different facet of their identity to their lecturers to the one which they presented to their friends. Many spoke about their professionalism in how they presented themselves publicly in the world of the academy.

> Sometimes, it's kind of pretending to know what they're [lecturers] talking about when they tell you about some theory or method. But really you might not be sure. So you go away and you look it up or you ask your friends about it and then when they [lecturers] mention it to you again you sort of say more and show that you really do understand it. You can't understand everything the first time.

Women's different constructions of their Asian identity were negotiated upon the different roles and circumstances. They negotiated several identities outside and inside the university environment. As Wenger states (1998:74): 'a shared practice thus connects participants to each other in ways that are diverse and complex'. Being included in what matters is in fact a requirement for 'being engaged in a community's practice, just as engagement is what defines belonging' (p77). Women wanted to feel included within their communities of practice. This did not stop them from being part of non-Asian friendship networks, but they emphasised that it was the Asian groups to which they felt they *belonged*. As Wenger (1998:160) argues, 'different ways of engaging in practice may reflect different forms of individuality'. The idea of 'pretending to know' was something that women would only reveal to members of their own communities of practice. Women felt they could trust and confide in women who were in comparable positions, juggling the expectations of home life with the world of the university and reinventing themselves to manage these different worlds.

Reconciling different identities requires 'the construction of an identity that can include different meanings and forms of participation into one nexus' (Wenger, 1998:162). As these women engage in their different communities of practice – their Asian and non-Asian friendships – and the academy, their identities encompass multiple perspectives in negotiating new meanings. It is within these new meanings that they can negotiate their new activities and identities, since 'an identity combines multiple forms of membership through a process of reconciliation across boundaries of practice' (Wenger, 1998:163). Thus, the process of attending university required significant re-flection upon their identity and re-evaluating how their lives fitted in with a wider group of people than the domestic and labour traditions of their parents would have demanded. One significant effect of their lives was that attending university itself othered them and did so in different ways to those they might have already experienced, such as being an ethnic minority woman living in a predominately white society.

Being othered in the Academy

Many of the women discussed how they felt 'distanced' from the university and the academic environment of higher education. They talked of their positioning as outsiders within the academy, as not fully belonging to the academy and not being *allowed* to belong because the Academy was white, middle class and male.

> If you look at all the lecturers and professors I would say they are mainly all white and most of them are men and they are all middle class. Because we are not seen in that way, we tend to be seen as separate to them. I think it's the same wherever you go, whether it's Oxford or here. It's mainly men who are in the higher positions and they are the ones with the power. It's hard if you're Asian or black and if you're a woman.

This outsider status and notion of 'otherness' distinguished some women as different and many found this particularly problematic. They repeatedly stressed their desire to fit in. One of the commonest reasons for choosing a local university was to make the process of fitting in easier. Women actively chose routes into university that they anticipated would minimise any traumatic upheaval or over-complications in their lives,

> I wanted to come here to study because it is my local university, it's where I live. It is easy for me to travel to and I thought there would be quite a few people from Asian backgrounds coming here and it would be mixed. I prefer that than going to a university that was all white or all black or Asian. If I went to a university that was all white, I would feel differently. I don't think I would feel as though I was part of it and I would stand out. Here it's not like that at all. It's also the area. You know that most of the people who go there probably live in this area.

> I think that most of the other Asian people are from the same sort of backgrounds like me, they are not just coming here after doing their 'A' levels, they may have taken some time out or some of them might be here as mature students and come through Access courses, like me.

Yet these anticipated easy options were only half realised. Once at university many of the respondents faced unexpected differences such as those which materialised in their relations with white middle class lecturers – an issue emphasised most by the mature women in the sample.

> We are different from the people who work in the university, they are seen as being part of the elite because they are part of an elite group. We are not really seen as part of that – we are opposite to that – we are not white, we are women and most of us don't come from the traditional middle class backgrounds. We are not the same as them.

It was the more mature women who understood and reflected upon how their otherness was contingent upon a number of factors, including class. Many accepted that class also influenced the type of universities they had selected in the first place,

> I am not saying there are no middle class Asian people, of course there are. They are the ones who go to the proper universities and they study medicine or law and not social sciences. But I do think that the type of university you want to attend is influenced by who else is also attending that university. You are more likely to want to go somewhere where you know that you will feel comfortable and be able to identify with the people rather than being seen as different to them.

Despite identifying with other students at the university, women felt a detachment from the university, an outsider status in which they did not identify with the structure of higher education as represented by their lecturers. They referred to this as the 'middle classness' of the university environment. Within the university, the boundaries of membership were not only for outsiders but also for insiders. These boundaries keep insiders in and outsiders out. Being a member of a community of practice has the advantage of offering engagement in a 'productive enterprise around which to negotiate diverging meanings and perspectives' (Wenger, 1998:114). It enabled women to cope with their outsider status of not being middle class and not being a member of the academic elite. Read et al (2003) found that minority ethnic students are more likely to feel they belong in institutions in which there are many others who are like them. Several of the respondents questioned the nature of the assessment procedures.

> The way the university system works is for people who know about it. If you look at the language and the assignments we have to do, it's ok if you're from a middle class background and understand it all. But if you're not then you're at a disadvantage. You have to work harder than other people who know the system. They may use words and language that a lot of us are not familiar with. Also some of us don't actually have people who we can ask because our parents and our siblings may not have gone to university. People who have parents and other people they can ask are immediately advantaged compared to us.

Women from non-traditional backgrounds who had entered university through Access courses indicated that higher education was not the norm in their background. One interpretation of their lives might be that they had been disadvantaged by leaving school early and maybe entering into the job market: but an alternative view would celebrate their accumulated life experiences and their determination to succeed in higher education later in life. This latter interpretation, whilst it may have influenced universities in selecting students, did little to make life at university any easier.

> A lot of us have come here as mature students and most of the people here have done access courses. We haven't left school at 18 and come here to university, we have worked and done other things and have realised that we need a degree if we want to get on in life. Our parents didn't go to university and some of our parents have no education.

Read *et al* (2003:71) noted that 'there was a feeling of 'isolation' rather than 'belonging': a feeling that is related to the culture of the academy itself rather than the make-up of the student body'. Many of the Asian women felt they belonged to their communities of practice, yet at the same time felt 'distanced' from the procedures, processes and structures of the academy. They coped with this distance and outsiderness by supporting and relying on each other and maintaining regular contact with members of their community of practice. In their eyes, the Academy was white, middle class and male and did not represent *them*. Their routes into higher education were either as mature students or via Access courses. Asian women came together in their communities of practice 'not only to engage in pursuing some enterprise but also to figure out how their engagement fits in the broader scheme of things' (Wenger, 1998:162). Yet despite the distance between the worlds of the Asian women and their perceptions of the academic world, their communities of practice created an environment in which they achieved their aspirations.

Family influence

If the new world of the Academy was understood as a space in which Asian women found themselves othered, the family might be expected to represent aspects of security and be a space where students could draw upon natural resources of belonging. Whilst this was largely the case, many of the women I spoke to also described not only the importance of their family's encourage-ment but also some of the tensions that arose as a result of their active parti-cipation in their studies. Typically, however, parents wanted their own daughters to succeed, even though they themselves did not have higher edu-cation qualifications.

> My parents want me to do really well at uni. They tell me it's very important for me to do well and they make allowances for that. They don't ask me to do anything in the house which they think will affect my studies. They know that if I do well, then I can get a good job. And I know that if I get a good job I can make decisions for myself.

Generally, both parents encouraged their daughters to achieve and succeed. They too expected that success in higher education would have a positive impact upon future positions in the labour market and the potential for higher income. The parent's own levels of education were generally fairly low and sometimes nonexistent and this contributed to a sense that education was even more important. Families actively looked to their children to better themselves; for children to be more successful than they had been. In the first instance, this was achieved by participating in education and later by em-barking upon secure and successful careers.

> Because my parents themselves aren't what you would call from a middle class background, they want me to do well. They push me hard and want me to do the best.

Education for these women was the more important for being something they had to work for and which would make a significant difference to both their professional and personal lives.

> I know that getting an education is so important to me. But it's also important to my parents because they know that it will make a difference to my life. I know that it will enable me to have more choices. If you don't have that education you would only have a few choices and that could influence the decisions that you make.

Many of the women said that that their family's support was even greater for them than for their brothers. There was a feeling that women had to strive consciously to be successful whereas the traditional role of being a bread-winner always compelled men to work hard,

> I think my parents push me harder than they do with my brother. They know he will do ok, because he will have to get a job no matter what. They want him to get a good job so want him to do well. With me, I could just easily drift along and not do so well and think that someone else can look after me. They [parents] don't want me to think like this, they want me to be able to look after myself.

Women's participation in higher education enhanced their status. Although being at university was often a difficult time because they did not feel at ease in the academic world, their success was often enabled by the support networks they could draw upon. Whilst some of the most effective support they received came from their peer group, that is other Asian women with similar backgrounds, it also came from the support networks they had at home and within their extended families. Family and community were initially very important in persuading them to enrol at university. Once there, their family and traditional communities, along with their new communities of practice helped them feel they could achieve, despite being an outsider.

> However, upon starting a degree course many women began to find new tensions arising because of becoming a student. Their identity in their home lives had inevitably to change. Some of the more mature students found it hard to fit in time to study with their everyday routines of contributing to domestic labour and the labour market.

> Even though I know it [going to university] is a good thing, it does get hard. My husband does tend to go on sometimes about the house not being clean enough and says that perhaps I should be working instead of studying. The time frame is long as well, it's three and maybe four years if I want to do more. I know he wants me to do it, but he doesn't want me to neglect other things.

This respondent also described the tensions caused by finding time to study, something for which she felt she did not receive much support.

> Finding the time to sit down and read and then write an assignment is quite hard. When you have a family and you have your home, it's your responsibility to make sure that everything is in order. All that stuff has to be done first and then I can sit down and do it. Then I am too tired to do it well. You need the time as well. You can't sit down for just 15 minutes and read something or write something. You need more time and sometimes you need a whole day to get stuck into the reading and the assignment. Sometimes I just don't have that

time and so have to do it in short spurts of time. Because of that I don't think I do as well as I could or as well as other people who perhaps don't have the commitments that I might have.

Several other mature students felt that although extended families were proud of them, there was also a feeling among them that the women were spending too much time studying.

Sometimes my husband's relatives will come over and when I'm studying they will say, 'oh she's studying again, does she never stop'. So I have to stop and speak to them. It's like they don't take it seriously enough. But if it was my husband I think that would be seen as different. Because it's me, they think my main role is to look after the house and the family and they think women should be a certain way so don't take my studying so seriously. If it was my husband they would take it more seriously because they think that's what he should be doing.

Many of the married women spoke about the sacrifices they made and how these sacrifices sometimes caused conflict in the family. There was some resentment that although an education might pay rich dividends in future, in the short-term they were bringing no income into the family home. Their careers appeared to be on hold, particularly if they were employed in low wage part-time work that sat more easily with other commitments rather than looking for a full-time job with an obvious developmental career path.

I know that I could be working properly – I am working part-time but that job is not a real job it is for the money only. My sister in law did say to me last week, 'why are you studying now, isn't it too late for you?' She thinks instead of wasting my time now I could be working full-time and earning money. But I tell her that I will be able to do this after the course has finished, but she does not understand. I want to get a job in which I feel valued and in which I feel fulfilled and you can only do that if you have a good education. I could get any other type of job like shop work or sewing but that isn't what I want to do. I want to do more than look after the house and be a wife and a mother, I want to have a career for me, [respondent's emphasis] it's important for me to have that.

This respondent told me about her husband's attitude towards her studying and his emphasising the importance of her traditional duties as a mother and wife in the here and now, rather than her potential in the future,

He sometimes thinks that I am wasting my time and my studying always comes last. He thinks I should be earning and he doesn't take it very seriously. His work comes first and the family comes first and my studying comes last. So I do have to compromise a lot.

Many of the married women in the study considered being married a disadvantage whilst at university. The disadvantages of being an Asian woman in a white middle class environment were compounded by the expectations of fulfilling traditional homemaker roles:

> It is better to do this studying when you are single and still at home with your parents because then you can concentrate on it. When you are married and working, your studies always come last and so you end up not giving them the time and attention they need. Also I think there are other things that have to come first like your role as a wife and a mother. Sometimes there have been seminars in the evenings I have wanted to go to, but have not been able to because my husband won't look after the kids or comes home late. These things add to the pressure of wanting to do well. But it make me want to succeed more so that I know when I finish I would have achieved something and will be able to do more with my life – whether that is getting a good job or going on to do more studying.

The tensions experienced by the women affected their success at university. The married women felt their studying was secondary to their role as wife and mother and consequently suffered. That many respondents had to do part-time work in order to supplement family income added pressure. For many married women the family's financial needs gave them little option other than to work and generate some income.

> I work part-time as well as studying. I have to work because my husband said he didn't want me to stop working so that I could study and also because we do need the money. That's also an additional pressure for me because it makes me tired when I know I have to go to work and then come back and do some reading for my course. But it all has to be done. There is a lot of pressure, if I wasn't going to work then it would still be hard, but it would make things a little easier because I wouldn't be so tired. But I wouldn't have the money that I have now and it would then be harder on my husband because he would be the only one who went to work.

Some of the unmarried respondents who worked also spoke about the pressure of working part-time. They saw work as an assertion of some independence from their families and proof that they could be both students and responsible members of their family.

> I work part-time because I think it helps my parents. They know then that I am getting some money that I can use for myself and I don't have to keep asking them for it all of the time. I don't mind working, but it can get tiring when you are

trying to do too much. Also I think my parents would be disappointed if I gave up my job, they would see that as really irresponsible. They want to support me, but also want me to take some responsibility for things as well.

However, despite these tensions and difficulties, the determination of the mature married women to succeed showed that what could have been potential disincentives to persevering with their studies spurred them on to prove other people wrong,

I have to carry on and I have to do well – or as well as I can. If I fail, then that means all the things that my husband and family have said will be true – it was too hard and I couldn't do it. But I am going to do it, but having more time could mean that I could do better than I probably will. I would never give it up and I will try hard not to fail. I think I will pass, but perhaps not as well as I would have liked to.

Many of the women related their experiences to their cultural backgrounds and appeared acutely conscious of their responsibilities in relation to their traditional lifestyles. They distinguished their lives and approach to studying from those of their non-Asian peers:

Being an Asian woman, being a Sikh woman I know that there are certain ways in which I have to behave and certain things that I have to do and that means I have to put my family first and my children first. Even though I know my husband and my family want me to do well, they still don't expect me to go out all night with all the other students and get drunk.

A Muslim respondent said she was similarly constrained by her cultural background and acknowledged the responsibilities it placed upon her:

There are certain things that we have to do first and that come first and they are your husband and your children. Then you can turn to the studying. Being Muslim I have to behave in a certain way and make sure that I don't do anything so that people could talk about me and say things about me.

Somewhat ironically, some younger unmarried respondents also spoke about how their families created pressures because they had given them the advantage of higher education. They described feelings almost of guilt that they should be allowed time to study whilst their parents or possibly elder siblings had never been allowed this luxury. Tied to this was the anxiety to do well in their studies; their family's expectations made them afraid to fail:

Because my mum gives me lots of time to study and knows that it is important, there is a lot of pressure on me to do well. For example I couldn't fail – that would be unheard of – they [my parents] would say, 'how can you fail when we have given you all this time to study and paid so much money for you to do the course?'

Another single respondent living at home spoke about having more time than women who were working part-time:

Because I am at home with my parents, there's so many things you take for granted, like I don't have to worry about doing the cleaning or the cooking if I don't want to. I know my mum will do that. I also don't have to worry about money or working like some of the people do here.

This relative sense of freedom was countered by her acute awareness of the pressure on her to succeed:

I do think there is a lot of pressure from parents for us to do well and we have to do well. There's the family name, because all my bigger family know that I'm at uni so I do have to do well. They would ask my parents and ask them what I got and what I was going to do after – so yes I do think there's a lot of pressure.

Overall, a pattern emerged of the family as both a site in which women were encouraged to participate in education and received support, but also as potentially problematic because of the pressures to conform to traditional homemaker roles – and to achieve. Married women in particular found themselves expected to fulfil all their household and social duties before they studied. Many also had to hold down part-time jobs in addition to studying and running a home. Whilst many of the respondents spoke about the support they received from their parents, this support was also associated with pressures to succeed. Many married women faced similar conditions attached to their education: because they were generating less income they were under pressure show they had not wasted their time at university.

Conclusions

We belong to and have changing relations with different communities at different times. These may be communities of practice amongst similar peer groups within the university environment or at home within more traditional ideas of community and family. This multimembership crosses different boundaries and different communities of practice. Asian women's identities and memberships include their roles as wives, mothers, daughters, members of an extended family and students. Being a member of more than one community of practice gives women a certain sense of their identity. The different communities of practice make different demands on women so they have to work to combine the university experience with their different identities.

Their behaviour has to be negotiated within their different communities of practice. As Wenger observes, 'the work of reconciliation may be the most significant challenge faced by learners who move from one community of practice to another' (1998:160). Women have to deal with conflicting forms of their individuality based on how it is defined in different communities of practice. Being a member of more than one community of practice – multi-membership – creates various tensions. Maintaining identity across different boundaries is not an automatic process and women have to work at it to find ways in which to integrate the different forms of participation. Within their communities of practice, women's identities encompass multiple perspectives in the negotiation of new meanings and within these new meanings women negotiate their identities between their different communities of practice. Clearly, young Asian women attending university confront challenges that are very different to those their parents and grandparents faced. By necessity, they are negotiating new identities and making adaptations to the expectations of both their traditional communities and their new academic circumstances.

6

Friendship networks and support

As is widely demonstrated by social scientists and psychologists, social support such as friendship and community networks is important for promoting good health and general well-being. Social support networks are crucial in coping with and managing stress and reducing the negative impact of stress in daily life. Support networks were crucial in managing the fears of the Asian women entering an alien environment and carrying with them great burdens of family expectations. The support networks amongst peers in the university who understood the stress of their new student lives and their home lives created a space in which new identities could be understood and strategies to manage their difficulties developed.

Most concepts of support identify two dimensions. One is about providing the individual with instrumental or practical assistance and the other relates to the benefits accrued in social interactions. Hobfoll and Stokes (1988:467) define social support as 'those social interactions or relationships that provide individuals with actual assistance or with a feeling of attachment to a person or group that is perceived as caring or loving'. This is also based on individuals seeking close caring relationships with others which give them a feeling of emotional security and well-being. The characteristics of the network such as size and frequency of interaction can lead to variations in the availability of social support resources. Measures of social support are based on frequency of contact between individuals, the quality of relationships and their impact on well-being and support resources (Cohen and Wells, 1985). Sarason *et al* (1987) regard the core underlying feature of measuring social support to be involvement in close, caring relationships which include regular contact (Sarason *et al*, 1987).

Cutrona (1986) developed measures of the various dimensions of support, such as network analyses and individual perceptions of support. Levels of social support are found to affect health and well-being both directly and indirectly. Many studies have found that social support enhances different aspects of subjective well-being and decreases levels of depression and psychological distress (cf Ensel and Lin, 1991). Social support can modify the impact of important life events and other stressors on health and well-being. It can act as a buffer and reduce the impact of life events and chronic strains on health and well-being (Cohen and Wells, 1985). Pugliesi and Shook (1998) found that social status can affect and shape support networks and their characteristics so that men from minority ethnic backgrounds generally have smaller social support networks and interact with them less often.

Social support resources

Social support resources are influenced by personal, social and environmental factors. For individuals to participate actively in networks, two factors have been identified as crucial: a sense of collective identity and a sense of collective agency (Klandermans, 1997). A sense of shared identity binds a group of people together while a sense of agency gives such networks purpose and makes them a useful project. Variation in support network characteristics such as resources can influence the facilitation and type of support available to each member of the network (Moore, 1990). Information, assistance and emotional support can be derived from informal networks.

The relationship between the social location of actors and networks can influence the provision of social support at any given time. Evidence suggests that differences in social support network characteristics relate to gender, employment, age and ethnicity (Moore, 1990). Major differences have been found in the size and composition of networks. Research shows that women are more likely to have larger support networks, with more frequent contact than networks shared by men (Burda et al, 1984). Women's support networks are also more likely than men's to be kin and friend centred (Hurlbert and Acock, 1990).

The level and types of social support available to individuals has also been linked to social class background. Brown et al (1975) have found that women from working class backgrounds were more likely to experience depression due to their lack of social support networks. This is often related to isolation and lack of regular contact with others. Turner and Noh (1983) observed that women from working class backgrounds who have little or no social support in their lives are less likely to have direct control over their lives regarding family and employment. Liem and Liem (1978) explain class and levels of social support by examining the impact of economic and financial stress on the lives of working class women.

Marriage has been identified as enhancing the availability of social support. Married people have greater access to kin relationships than unmarried people (Kessler and Essex, 1982) and are more likely to turn to their spouses for support. Parenthood has also been found to have a direct effect on the availability of social support resources (Pugliesi, 1989), as children can lead to new friends through contact with neighbours and other parents (Moore, 1990). Those with very young children, however, are likely to have less access to social support networks than those with children of school age (Leslie and Grady, 1985).

Age has also been shown to influence the size and composition of social support networks which decrease with age. The youngest and oldest individuals are more likely to have access to kin related social support networks and older women tend to have larger social support networks than older men, whose networks dwindle as they turn to their wives for support (Moore, 1990).

Few studies have examined the impact of ethnicity on social support networks. Campbell and McLean (2002) argued that through participation in social networks, those from socially excluded groups can construct their identities in ways which challenge their marginalised status and help improve individual life circumstances. Thus, social identities and participation in social support networks can serve as mechanisms for social change.

Marsden (1997) identified differences in network size, composition and ethnic heterogeneity amongst those from Black Caribbean backgrounds. Black respondents reported smaller social support networks compared to white respondents and the size of the social support networks was related to their educational background. The size of social support networks for Black respondents was higher amongst those with high levels of education (Everard *et al*, 2000).

Clearly, then, there are numerous variables that shape social networks in people's lives. Age, gender, class and ethnicity are all intertwined, exerting different pressures upon each other. Also clear is that social networks change over time and in relation to different circumstances. Asian women who left school at eighteen to work in a factory have a different experience of social networks from those attending university. This partly explains the importance of social networks: although they might be reactive and enable groups of similarly situated people to react to the daily pressures of their lives, they also have a generative function. That is to say, social networks do more than merely provide a response to lessen stress – they are at the heart of identity production. Members of these networks are looking to reconcile their past with their present lives and in so doing map out their potential futures.

Asian women and social support networks

Friendship networks provide support for women, both inside and outside educational institutions, and help them find mechanisms for success within higher education (Bhopal, 2008). Seth (1995) has argued that Asian women in higher education are disadvantaged compared to women from other minority ethnic groups. Asian women are seen as being burdened by their 'culture' and 'familial pressures' in which they are expected to be obedient and passive, and to enter into a 'forced' or arranged marriage (Afshar, 1994; Bhopal, 2009; Wilson, 2006). Consequently there is little useful outside or institutional support for Asian women and this in turn reinforces the negative stereotype of their being inward-looking and reliant upon family support. Whilst family support is generally readily forthcoming, it might not be as helpful, objective or as knowledgeable as, for example, that of a careers advisor who has professional expertise about educational options.

Research shows that Asian parents want their children to succeed in education so push them towards success while providing a supportive environment (Anwar, 1998). Whilst Bhatti's (1999) research indicated gender differences in the support provided and that mothers are more likely than fathers to want their daughters to succeed academically, Ahmad (2003) showed both parents, regardless of their gender or their own educational experiences, want their children to succeed in higher education. Ahmad argued that Asian fathers are more likely to be positive about the education of their daughters and see that success in higher education can enhance success in the labour market. This possibly marks a shift in the value attached to women being educated within Asian culture or it may be a consequence of changing economic realities. It does, however, clearly challenge some of the stereotypes popularly attributed to Asian women.

Bell and Coleman (1999) explored the importance of friendship networks for understanding social relations through the process of migration in which friendship networks can vary cross-culturally. Individuals from migrant communities are more likely to develop stronger ties with others who have experienced similar processes of migration. The importance and relevance of kinship support networks has also been identified by Werbner (1990) in her study of male Pakistani migrants and by Shaw's work on Pakistanis in Bradford (2000). Friendship networks have been identified as providing support for young people from minority ethnic backgrounds in the work of Alexander (2000) and Baumann (1996). Little research, however, has explored the focus of female friendships in Asian communities, as it is assumed that support is provided by kin support networks rather than friends (Palriwala and Risseeu, 1996). In my discussions with Asian women at university, it was apparent that although family networks remained important and integrated within their lives, in the new setting of the university increasing importance was attached to informal friendship networks.

Understanding the social support networks of migrant communities is related to notions of belonging and attachment. Mand (2006) has argued that Asian communities have varying experiences of migration and kinship and consequently cultural and familial experiences differ *within* and *between* the groups. Such differences affect the different types of networks individuals become involved in and those which they turn to for support. Mand's research demonstrates how Asian families in Britain are not necessarily self-sufficient units which are bound together by tradition and custom, but rather that some members of the communities prefer to live independently from their family and make their own decisions. Friendships for Asian women were related to different stages in their life course, but all women valued their friendships for providing them with a valuable social support network.

Little research has examined the importance of friendship networks for South Asian women, focusing instead on relationships within family and kin networks. Research on friendships and minority ethnic women is often related to the study of gender, rather than the relevance and importance of social support networks and their role in individual's lives. The second half of this chapter looks at women's social support networks and examines women's engagement in their social support networks as part of their engagement in their community of practice in higher education. Whilst the traditional sense of community associated with family and home life has not been abandoned, new ideas of what constitutes community are being generated. In particular, when faced with new and different challenges associated with balancing university life with more traditional commitments, communities of practice develop amongst Asian women in order to support themselves and to propagate collegiate strategies to succeed.

Friendship networks amongst Asian women: communities based upon similarity

Many of the participants in my study had friends from similar backgrounds, that is amongst Asian women who shared their understanding of what home life and culture entailed. Having friendship networks in which women could identify with others in the university who were like them, gave them a sense of security. Their shared background formed part of their community of practice and was fundamental to how this worked. Identification with others was crucial for the community of practice to function in an environment in which women generally felt different to those around them. The friendship networks reinforced and strengthened the community of practice for women and confirmed their sense of belonging within it. Many of the women emphasised the importance of having friends and what this meant to them.

> It's really important to have friends because they can help you when you need them and they are always there for you.

> You know who your friends are because they are the ones who support you and they are the ones you know that you can rely on. In this kind of environment [university] when you are sometimes under pressure to get your assignments done and all the reading, if you have people you can rely on then that makes a big difference to your experience and time at university.

Another respondent emphasised the strength her friendships gave her and suggested that having friends at university changed her approach to university attendance. Going to university was important for seeing her friends and not just to study,

> When I know I am coming to uni [university] I know that I will be able to see my friends and I know that I will be able to speak to them about things that I may need some support for and they will be here for me and that is the most important thing for me – to know that they are here for me.

Being a member of a friendship network was regularly described as a source of security. It meant they could turn to their friends for help, advice and support when they needed it. This was crucial for women who found the university a very unfamiliar environment in which they felt actively marginalised and understood as 'outsiders' or 'others'. The idea that the ethos of the university tended to anticipate a different type of student to themselves was expressed by many respondents. They felt that universities were established for white, middle class students rather than Asian women and one consequence was that Asian women were marginalised throughout the working practices of the Academy. It was one of the reasons why women felt they wanted to belong to a group of women with whom they could identify. One explained the importance of a collective identity amongst her friends:

> Having friends is not just about having friends, it's about having friends who are like you, it's about having friends who understand you. If someone is from the same group as you, then they understand what you are going through and they understand that you may have the same sort of experiences as them. If I wanted to speak to my friends about some things that I thought were sensitive like racism or something at home I know I can tell my friends and they will listen to me and not judge me. This is because they probably have been through similar experiences as me and so could identify with me. There are certain things that you can say to certain people who will accept what you are saying and there are other things that you can't say. You know what you can say to your friends and you know they will be there for you.

Being a member of a community of practice gave women connections that engendered a sense of belonging. Making friends with other women who were like themselves created an environment in which they could feel accepted. They created groups in which women felt secure and comfortable and thus a space to discuss issues that were personal and sensitive to them and which they would not discuss with non-Asian women. The empathy of friends who had similar experience of issues such as racism or family matters was vital to establish trusting mutual understanding.

Several women told me that one consequence of being marginalised within the university environment was that it virtually forced them to want friendships with women who were like them. They were far more proactive in seeking out friends and communities of practice as students than they would have been in their general lives.

> I want to be friends with people who are like me and who understand my experiences. This means that I'm more likely to choose women, say Asian women to be my friends because I know they will understand things about me that other non-Asian women may not, so I'm more likely to make sure my friends are people like me.

> I get on better with other Asian women because they have similar views as me and they have also had similar experiences as me and we can talk about those. It's kind of knowing that there is an empathy there, with your life and some of the things that you have in your culture. This is something we can share with each other when we come to uni.

The active pursuit of friendship networks and communities of practice highlights the adaptations Asian women make to university life and also how being a member of a community of practice is related to the exercise of agency. Asian women don't simply gravitate towards a community of practice, they actively seek out like-minded students in order to create their own communities.

Different friendship networks between Asians and non-Asians

Many of the women were also friends with people from different backgrounds to themselves. But when they described these friendships they seemed not to understand them in the same terms of communities that they associated with friendship networks amongst Asian women. One woman described her other friends, thus:

> I do have other friends as well. I am friends with some black women and men and also white women and men here. But I think those friendships are different. I don't know if I would speak to them if something was happening at home or about racism or something like that. It would depend how close I felt to them. To my black friends I would speak to them about racism, but I'm not sure if I would to my white friends. They are different to us and we are different to them. They do see us as being different.

The differences she describes here are related primarily to skin colour and ethnicity. The nuanced suggestion that racism might be discussed with a Black person but not a white person ought to suggest that having experienced racism and discrimination was a defining factor for being a member of a community of practice with people like themselves. But in fact the sense of otherness and of possibly being in a hostile environment was not enough on its own for these friendships to coalesce into the stronger and more supportive communities of practice. Above and beyond the shared understandings of racism, it was necessary for women to come from the same cultural backgrounds. They might share many different life experiences based upon typical traits such as age, gender or skin colour and it was possible to empathise in part with other people's lives. But without the shared cultural background, the bond within the friendships they made seemed to be weaker. The daily engagement in their community of practice became part of Asian women's experience of higher education. It went beyond the friendship expressed more generally between Asian women and other students.

Some of the women had exclusively Asian women friends, but most did not. What was clear, however, was that they attached different levels of importance to their friendships. Identification with women similar to themselves was something they valued and wanted to hold on to. They felt comfortable discussing personal familial issues such as arranged marriages with other Asian women because they had a shared knowledge and could advise them in a realistic fashion that took account of their commitments to family life. Discussing such issues with non-Asian women was much harder because it was felt there was at best a lack of understanding about their lives, and at worst, that these people might have stereotypical notions about their lives.

> I do feel as though I am accepted within my group of Asian friends and I do feel that makes me feel quite safe and not worried about things that I may worry about if I was not part of their group or on my own. I am glad I have this group of friends that I know will accept me and not judge me or see me as being different to them. There are cultural things that they understand about me and my family like about marriages and some of the customs that we have.

> Some of the other women, like the white women do have sort of ideas about us. They think that we have to do what our parents tell us all the time and that we have no choice in our lives. They get those assumed ideas from what they see on the TV or what they read and those are just stereotypes, they are not true. But some people believe those things.

Whilst all friendships were valued, the strongest bonds for Asian women were with one another. They felt that non-Asian women might possibly have offensive or derogatory ideas about some aspects of their culture and particularly that stereotyped notions about Asian women would form part of their non-Asian peers' preconceptions about them. That Asian women students felt unable to engage with these other students suggests they are subject to an undertow of racism amongst the wider student population and that these views reflected the wider positioning of Asian women within the Academy. That is to say, that the non-Asian students would share with their lecturers ideas that mark Asian women out as not belonging within the world of academia. Alternatively, we might view these Asian women as rejecting the opportunities open to all students to meet and mix with new and different peers. Their forming and adherence to new insular community groupings of people like themselves in a way creates a mirror of their family and kinship networks. This process could easily be read as evidence confirming the stereotypical views of Asian women as quiet, keeping themselves to themselves and irrevocably tied to the patriarchal structures of their traditional communities.

Yet the picture that emerged from my research challenges both these interpretations. It suggests instead that the relationships being created are fluid and reflect the need for Asian women to make adaptations that foster security and comfort in their lives. Being friendly with many different people was quite different from the specific bonding that occurred within the communities of practice the women developed, and was one of the consequences of attending university. They did indeed grasp the opportunity to talk to and befriend people unlike those they might have expected encountering before they went to the university. The experience was not unique to Asian women students, but Asian women faced real differences that distinguished them from all other students. Although some might discuss racism with Black students but not white because the Black students would in all likelihood have experienced racism, this was not the full story. Only some of the racism encountered by Asian women, such as name-calling, would be similar. Other racisms they encountered in student life were specifically related to being *Asian* and to being an *Asian woman*. The expectations around issues such as arranged marriages and cultural stereotypes such as patriarchal family lives had a huge impact on the expectations held of them by the Academy. Asian women were expected to live within an Asian 'bubble' in which their responses to racism or to the prevalence of white middle class lecturers or to the clash of home and student life were articulated in the culture of Academia in a simplistic and predictable fashion. Asian women would for example be expected never to challenge a lecturer. They *would* be expected suddenly to drop out of a course because they had been flown back to the sub-continent by relatives intent on marrying them to a villager twice their age. The unpredictability of Asian women's responses was best illustrated by how they dealt with such stereotyping: they created communities of practice, close-knit groups in which Asian women could circulate their own interpretations of their lives and prioritise successful strategies to complete their education.

Ongoing communication

For many of the women, frequent face-to-face communication helped to influence how the community was perceived by its members. Having regular informal meetings such as at coffee breaks in the canteen or meeting in the library, sitting together in lectures and seminars and lunching together positively reinforced the membership of the community and the effective collaboration existing within it.

> I know they [my friends] will be there for me when I need them. We always arrange to meet each other when we know we're going to be here. We meet in

the canteen and we have coffee together and then we go to lectures together and we go to the library. Meeting like this is good for us, because we know we are there for each other, we can chat about things. I suppose it sort of makes you feel secure when you know you are with friends you can trust and rely on.

The impact of these networks went beyond simply thinking about how best to cope with the stresses and pressures of balancing student and home life. It enhanced success in tackling academic work and provided opportunities for students to support each other in developing their academic thinking. There was an interesting link between the stress associated with fearing failure and the impact this would have within their families. By engaging with communities of practice, a support network developed that not only shaped their university lives but also increased their comfort in their home lives. The familiarity that was so crucial in bonding Asian women together to deal with the difficulties of university extended much further. One respondent, for instance, indicated that the familiarity and regular meetings with her friends supported her and helped with doing assignments.

The meetings we have are really good for me because I am the sort of person who needs to talk about the work, I can't just go away and do it. So when we meet we usually talk about the assignments we have to do and if one of us doesn't understand it then we all try and help that person, so we work together like a team really. We look after each other. That works well for someone like me and I really do think that if I didn't have the chance to talk to my friends about the assignment, I don't think I would have passed or done as well as I have. It's having the confidence to say to your friends that you don't understand something and you know they won't laugh at you but will support you. Some of them have also said they don't understand things or find things hard, then we support each other.

The subtext of this comment is that without her close network of friends she would have no one to confide in about the practicalities of course work, neither within the university nor, more critically, in her home life. With her close friends, this respondent was identifying boundaries between home, the Academy and her community of practice within the university. It was only here that she was developing the potential to push back boundaries and re-shape her identity. This was reshaping identity in the very real sense of engaging with the education system, gaining new experiences and shaping her potential opportunities in the future. The meetings were an ongoing process related for women who were members of the same community of practice for the duration of their course. The ongoing communication helped reinforce the shared practices within the communities. As Wenger (1998) argued, identity is negotiated and marked out at the boundaries between whether or not one belongs.

Some of the women experienced their belonging within their community of practice through the specific support they received from the community members:

> For me, it's the regular meetings and chats that we have. It's important to know that we can support each other no matter what we are going through. It's that I know the other Asian girls will understand and that makes a big difference to whether you feel that you are supported or accepted in the group. If there is an issue or a problem, we know that we will see other so we can talk about it. We usually see each other a lot in the week so get the chance to chat and work together on assignments.

This support was crucial in times of need, such as when deadlines had to be met or when their home situation became tense and stressful. These support networks enabled the women to experience their selves in an environment in which they felt understood, secure and safe.

> I know there are things that I can just discuss with my friends here. I know they will understand things about the culture that I wouldn't have to go into detail or explain to them – like I would for other women who were not Asian. So that does make it easier to talk to someone about the things that you are going through. If they are from the same cultural group as you and they have similar experiences then you know you can identify with each other and you know you can get support from each other. Sometimes these kinds of things can make a difference to how you choose your friends and who they are.

The environment they created was for many of the women the only one in which they could discuss all the personal aspects of their lives as students.

Conclusions

Engaging in their communities of practice in higher education enabled the women to receive support from their friendship networks. They formed friendship networks among Asian and non-Asian students and the different networks provided different kinds of support. Women were able to identify with their Asian friends and could speak to them about familial and sensitive issues which they felt non-Asian friends might not understand. They received a different kind of support from their non-Asian friends, frequently asso-ciated with seeking alternative friendships in which they could relax and escape from their familial and cultural pressures.

The women's friendships in their communities of practice can be understood in relation to social capital. The idea of social cohesion in communities has generated interest in social capital (Putnam, 2000). Putnam refers to 'bonding ties' as interactions between members of a group that build and maintain cohesion and solidarity and 'bridging ties' – the interactions external to the group. These terms are used to understand the concept of social capital: resources that are made available to individuals or groups by virtue of networks and their associated norms and trust (Portes, 1998). Putnam (2000) suggests that social capital in the form of networks of trust facilitate cooperation for mutual benefit. Other writers (Coleman, 1988; Cox, 1998) discuss social capital as a public good enabling greater output from the physical and human capital available. Kilpatrick *et al* (1999) argue that social capital has an important role in influencing and sustaining an environment which is ready to adapt and change. They assert that the process of learning occurs in the context of the social capital of the community in which the individual, group or organisation learns (1999:131).

Putnam (1993) defined social capital as networks – where individuals have high levels of participation in their local community groups – and norms – in which there are high levels of trust and reciprocity amongst group members. The network dimensions of Asian women's friendships can be used to explain why they form and take part in them. Through their social capital, women can build their friendships, and these are not necessarily exclusive to Asian women. Through their communities of practice as well as their friendship networks, Asian women can come together to find support at the university which enables them to cope with and challenge their marginalised status. The women in my study saw their close and supportive friendships as an important part of being a member of the community of practice in higher education.

The personal networks that women were engaged in were concentrated and located in and around the university environment. When the women spoke about their exclusion at school, in the workplace or in the university environment, they found a sense of inclusion in their friendship networks. They identified with these networks because these represented their needs and interests and consequently enabled the women to support each other collectively and individually. The frequency of interaction between the women strengthened the cohesion of the friendship networks.

The women had regular contact with each other and felt they could rely on their friends. Through the development of trust and shared values they gained much from their friendship networks. Through their identity as Asian women and their knowledge of higher education the women contributed to their community of practice. Regular face-to-face interaction strengthened the friendship networks and accumulated social capital. Engaging within the community of practice strengthened friendship networks and so reduced the chances of isolation. Whilst bridging social capital was evident, far greater emphasis was placed upon the importance of developing bonding social capital. Like many marginal groups, these women attached particular importance to establishing a defensive bonding that first and foremost provides security in an insecure world and allows them to further strengthen their positions.

7

Families and financial support

Family support for education encompasses a multitude of elements, from parental encouragement to attend and persist with studies, to specific advice about what institutions and what courses are best. The wider network of grandparents, aunts, uncles, brothers and sisters may also be involved and they will probably reflect their own expectations and previous involvement in higher education. Though clearly important, such support appears nebulous. It is measurable only in subjective and intangible terms of family 'ethos', 'hopes' or 'expectations'. Far more tangible is the level of financial support given to the student by the wider family. Since the introduction of student loans and tuition fees, the debts incurred by students in higher education has hugely increased. So the financial support and incentives a family can provide are often the determining factor in whether the family member can attend university.

Financial problems have been identified as a key reason for students dropping out of higher education (Davies and Elias, 2003). The amount of debt incurred by different types of students is strongly linked to their family background (Callender and Wilkinson, 2003). Students from non-traditional backgrounds such as mature, working class and minority ethnic students are likely to incur greater debts. Indeed, the financial risk incurred by having to take out a loan to attend university may well deter them in the first place (Christie and Munro, 2003). For poorer students the prospect of incurring debt can be both a deterrent and later a cause of stress if they do go to university.

Mature students, and particularly those with family commitments, are often compelled to calculate what the impact of lost earnings in the short term and of incurring debt in the medium term will have on their family's living standards. For a family who may be struggling or just about managing to house, feed and clothe themselves and their children, the loss of one person's full-time income may be too much to bear, even though the financial advantages associated with higher qualifications would ultimately far outstrip that earlier loss of earnings. Calculations of this kind reinforce the localism of non-traditional students described earlier. Living at home with their parents and attending their local university is a way to minimise costs. Mature Asian women with families who attend their local university may be able to retain links with local work opportunities, reduce the need for childcare and generally avoid upheaval and the costs that would be incurred.

Ethnic and class differences

For many Asian students, like working class students, staying at home is the best and cheapest option. Although the intention of student loans is to make available a source of funding for anyone to attend university, many working class and minority ethnic families find the prospect of incurring large debts very uncomfortable and groups who have no experience of family members attending university may be dubious about the potential for higher education to deliver higher earnings in the future. They may see the up-front debt of attending university as at best a gamble on their children's futures or at worst burdening them with a debt they cannot repay. Ethnic differences have been found in the decision to take out loans at all. Muslim students, for instance, are unlikely to take out student loans and consequently more likely to live at home with their parents (Callender and Kemp, 2000; Callender and Wilkinson, 2003).

Social class also affects the amount of debt incurred by students who do take out loans. Working class students are more likely to be in greater debt and take out larger loans (Callender and Kemp, 2000) and tend to leave university with large debts (Callender and Jackson, 2005). Students from middle class backgrounds are likely to receive greater financial support from their parents so generally leave university with smaller debts. So working class students face a double bind: they are less willing to take out a student loan but when they have to, the loan they need is generally greater. This affects the initial choice about which institution to attend and also reinforces fears about the potential burden of debt anticipated when going on to higher education.

Ahier *et al* (2000) found that all parents face financial pressure if their children decide to attend university, whether they can support their children financially or whether their children decide to remain at home whilst they complete their studies. Just as parents from different classes face different consequences in their support of their children, class and social capital also affect the decisions children make about pursuing higher education and the institutions they choose (Christie and Munro, 2003). Although student loans offer an opportunity to enter higher education, the choices for poorer families are more limited. The choices Asian families who hope their children will enter university have to make reflect wider societal shifts associated with the establishment of new universities, the move from grants to loans as the primary source of student funding and the increased number of people attending university.

Studying and working

Many studies have revealed an increase in the numbers of students who are compelled to work term time to support their studies (Forsyth and Furlong, 2003). Callender and Wilkinson (2003) found, that students from lower social class backgrounds were more likely to work during term time than those from higher social class backgrounds. And as Moreau and Leathwood (2006) found, working class students suffer greater financial hardship when attending university and many simply have to stay in paid employment to survive and complete their course. As students have reported, working whilst studying generally has a detrimental effect on academic achievement (Barke *et al*, 2000). The impact of term-time work has many obvious disadvantages: students have less time to study (Winn and Stevenson, 1997), suffer from tiredness (Buie, 2000), are more likely to miss lectures (Meyer, 2001), and find it harder to manage their time effectively (Broadbridge *et al*, 2000). The only studies which found positive correlations between term-time paid employment and academic performance were in situations where the employment was directly related to students' courses (McKechnie *et al*, 1998).

The importance of family support

Many of the women cited their families as providing the most significant support networks. All of the women indicated that their families encouraged them to attend university and to succeed once they were there. The support they received came from all sections of their family – mothers, fathers, siblings and their extended family. Many of the women cited their fathers as being very encouraging about their success at university. This section explores the range of financial and familial support women in the study received and the impact such support had on their engagement in their community of practice in higher education.

> Both of my parents are very supportive of me going to university, they want me to do well and they want me to be successful. They are both very supportive, if anything it is my dad who seems to push me harder. He really wants me to do well, he wants me to get a good education so that I don't have to struggle. He also knows that when I decide to get married I will want to go out to work and he wants me to get a good job and not to struggle like he has. I think he also feels that he wants me to be independent and to be able to look after myself because he knows that times have changed now and lots of Asian women are independent now and want to rely on themselves to be successful.

The impact of migration and the upheaval within recent family history significantly influenced the support families gave to their daughters to enter higher education. Most parents had made the transition from the sub-continent to Britain in the hope of improving the financial security of the family and many felt it had been difficult to establish themselves in a new country. Having struggled to do so, they wanted their children's lives to be different and to see their daughters succeeding without having to face similar struggles. One way to make their daughters' lives easier and more secure was to help them achieve some independence and security through higher education. Getting a degree was a gateway to earning an independent income and not being reliant on traditional patriarchal Asian structures or on the low-paid jobs many of their parents had to do in the British job market. As one of the respondent explained:

> My parents often tell us that when they came to this country they didn't have good jobs and they still work very hard now. So they want us to do better and want us to have better jobs than they had. They had to work in factories and they still do, they always say to me and my sisters that they want us to not work as hard as they had to. They want us to use our minds and not our hands. They had to struggle when they first came here and they don't want us to do that, so it's important for them that we succeed and do well.

Succeeding in their academic careers would enable the women to achieve jobs in the professional and managerial sector rather than taking on manual labour jobs as their parents had done. They emphasised that their parents encouraged them to succeed, mothers and fathers alike.

> They [parents] want us all to do well. They want us all to do well, the boys and the girls. These days women are getting on and doing very well. Lots of Asian women are now supporting their families. It has changed, it didn't used to be like that. The woman would stay at home and the man would go out to work. Roles are more divided and shared now. It's the same in our Indian families as

well. Lots of women seem to be in more powerful jobs now. Even if they get married and have a family women still want to be successful and get a good job. That's why parents know that their children want to do more with their lives even if they get married and have a family.

The support women received from their families varied. Some were able to speak to parents and siblings about their courses and their university experiences; some received support within the home, such as being excused from domestic chores and familial roles. Again this reflected a shift away from the patterns of family life associated with their parents' lives when they first migrated to Britain. Although there were some constraints in attending university, such as the localism, Asian families' values concerning education were shifting towards a more middle class outlook in which higher education is an expected and probable prospect for their daughters. The benefits they would gain by attending university were becoming embedded within social expectations.

> Because my parents know how much course work I have to do, they never ask me to do anything at home. They want me to do well and so I make sure I do well. They give me the time so I don't want to let them down. I do help in the home though as well, but my parents tell me to do my work first. It hasn't always been like that. I have older cousins who had to do all the housework and they had to study and they were expected to do well, but they didn't have as much time as we do nowadays to study. These days, parents say put your studies first and let us do the rest. They feel that them helping us will be better for us in the long term so that we can do well. They don't want us to fail, so they do what they can to help us. When we do succeed they are very proud and know they have played a big part in our success and how well we have done. I appreciate the support I get from my family.

Another respondent said she was excused from attending family functions, and that this was a complete break from family tradition.

> If I don't want to go to visit family or if there's a family function and I have an assignment I need to finish, my parents tell me that I don't have to go. They don't worry about whether people will say why I haven't come. They want me to do well. It also depends on what the family function is and how important it is. If it's a wedding then of course I wouldn't miss that, but other things I would. If I have an assignment that needs to be done then that is the first priority and my parents do also put pressure on me to put my studies first and I don't want to let them down as well. You know as well that you want to do it for yourself but because your parents have invested so much time and money as well you don't want to waste that, you want to do well so you make more of an effort.

At the same time, many of the women indicated that when they did attend functions, they saw them as a source of support. Reflecting the wider shifts within Asian communities, they knew they were not unique in their experiences but that others too were entering higher education. At functions women met with their extended kin and shared their experiences of attending university. Exchanges of their experiences emphasised the positive support women received from extended kin networks.

> Meeting at family functions is a good thing because you see all your family and your cousins and it sort of has a familiarity to it. You feel you are with people that you belong to and people that will understand you. When I see my cousins here we can all talk about what it's like at uni and we know that we are all under the same kind of pressure from our parents and our families, but at the same time we sort of see them as being our main sources of support, because we need them and we know that we couldn't do it without them. Seeing other members of my extended family like my cousins who are going through the same sort of thing gives me a different kind of support.

The novelty of being the first generation to attend university meant that the experience was an unknown quantity, one that came loaded with concerns and fears. It was, moreover, associated with other people's lifestyles and social capital, particularly those of the white middle class. So exchanges in the community and extended family provided a sense of familiarity and security that was doubly useful. Not only did the women meet people who shared similar experiences, but they also enjoyed the security of being amongst a well-understood and sympathetic community.

> When I am with the family and in the community, I do feel safe. It's because we are all the same, we are all trying as hard as we can to do well and our parents want us to well. People are supportive, they are not so competitive as they were once.

Many of the women reported also receiving financial support. This was vital: without it many would have been unable to pursue higher education. Being able to live at home and not being expected to contribute to the household income significantly enhanced women's experiences at university. Many worked part-time so as to contribute to their expenses but others indicated that this was not expected by their parents.

> I think a lot of Asian parents support their children financially. I am lucky and I know my friends are all in the same position as me. I don't have to contribute financially, I don't have to pay any rent or money for bills or food. I do ask my

parents if they want me to, but they refuse. They see it as their role to look after me and they want me to do well and don't want me to have to worry about money.

One interesting theme that emerged in many conversations was the feeling that parental support for children to attend university reflected the more general patterns of Asian family traditions. So even though respondents might be clear about how their circumstances differed from those of older siblings and cousins and how they were the first in their family to attend university – and not withstanding the patriarchal family expectations around the traditional role of women, they still conceptualised the support they received for attending university as typical of Asian families.

For us Asian people it's acceptable for us to live at home and not have to contribute financially for money or food. That isn't something we do in our culture. If you have children, we think you should look after them and support them. If my parents didn't support me financially, it would be very difficult for me to do this degree. I couldn't afford to go to university on my own and I couldn't afford to live on my own. I consider myself very fortunate that I can live at home and that my parents have helped me with my fees and that I don't have to worry about paying bills. If you have these additional worries as well as trying to pass the course then this must be a lot of pressure.

Financial support was delivered within a traditional framework. The women did not receive a sum of money in lieu of a student loan or the promise of assistance with their finances should they move away from home. Instead, financial support was delivered within the home. Whereas white middle class families might support their children financially to leave home to attend university, for most Asian students attending university was an extension of their childhood and adolescent domestic arrangements. Cultural notions of financial support were related to looking after one's family – but within the established patterns of family life. In addition to financial support, many of the women's networks of contacts and support were drawn from amongst their community and extended kin. Thus they drew upon the familiarity and comfort associated with relying on people they knew well. The importance of localism was also raised through family and community networks which were often located close by.

Family relationships

One area of support from within the family network deserves close scrutiny: the importance, as described by the women, of sibling relationships. They saw support from siblings as crucial in determining their success in higher education, specifically the older ones who had themselves experienced higher education. The women also encouraged their younger siblings and helped them with homework and projects.

> My older brother is doing his Masters degree now and he has been through doing the degree and he understands how hard it is, he thinks that I should work hard now so that it isn't too hard at the end. He supports me a lot and he sometimes reads my assignments for me so that they make sense – if he has the time. We support each other. He asks me to look at his work too.

Support from within the family added to the pressure to succeed. This often came from parents but some older siblings also made their expectations of them known.

> We do get a lot of support from our families and I don't want to let my parents or my family down. They think it's really important for me to do well and I think it's important for me to do well. So I make sure I understand what is being said in lectures and do what I can. I ask people for help and I make an effort.

Another respondent also said this support created pressure, albeit indirectly. Although her parents did not articulate their expectations of what she should achieve, she was conscious of the support she received and the pressure she felt because she did not want to let her parents down. Her burden seems heightened by the understanding that she has been given better opportunities than she might have had or even anticipated ten years ago.

> Sometimes it can be a bit suffocating because your parents are always helping and giving you time and stuff and you really feel that you have to do well. And if you don't that's a burden and you feel you have let them down. Also my older brother is really bright and has done very well so there is an expectation on me to succeed and do as well as him. That is an additional pressure as well.

So support worked as a double-edged sword. On the one hand, women saw it beneficial that they did not have to worry about where their next meal was coming from or whether they could pay the rent. On the other hand, this support created a great deal of pressure to do well. One woman described her negative feelings about some of the support she received and the additional burden it place upon her to do well,

> Although the support can be seen as negative and as a pressure, but at the same time it could be a good thing because it makes you want to *do well* [respondent's emphasis]. It sort of forces you to do well because you don't want to

let anyone down. So what happens is that you make your parents happy and proud, but you feel good at the same time. They would be really disappointed if I went to university for three years and after all that time and money they would have invested in me then I failed. That would be awful and it would also be embarrassing as well. When people would ask them they would have to say I have failed and they would not want that. They want us to do well.

The feeling that failure at university would have repercussions throughout her family and community networks was reiterated by another woman:

I want to do well, but my parents want me to do well *more* than I do [respondent's emphasis]. They have also invested a lot of money into my education. They give me lots of support and help me in whichever way they can. I failed a few of my assignments but was able to do them again, but was very disappointed. I didn't tell my parents, although I don't think they would have said anything, but they may have been disappointed. I did pass them in the end and I know I will get my degree. I want to please my parents and make them feel that their support has been worth it.

Many of the women spoke about wanting to please their parents, but also about how they wanted to do well for themselves and their hopes of future success in the job market. Their commitment to education enabled them to look forward to enhanced career paths.

Conclusions

Asian women received much of their social and financial support from their immediate and extended kin networks. The boundaries of each community were based on explicit markers such as family membership, and their involvement was understood in terms of attending weddings and family functions. Whilst these were supportive environments generally, engagement with the family and wider community was associated with pressure created by expectations about succeeding at university and the dread of the consequences if they failed. Despite these pressures, the women actively worked to maintain their family and community links; the advantages and strengths associated with their community clearly outweighed the disadvantages. Their involvement in communities of practice at university formed with similar women can be understood as one means of protecting the general support of family and home life whilst at the same time acknowledging and coping with the stress evoked by remaining within traditional community boundaries.

The distinction between the experience of community that Asian women took with them to university and the new communities of practice they developed at university can seem fairly marginal. There is some overlap between 'community' and 'communities of practice' and both work in a similarly supportive fashion. Wenger (1998) argues that it is within different 'boundary objects' such as accommodation that communities of practice can manifest themselves. Some Asian women spoke about finding support through the social and cultural networks at their local Gurdwara or Mosque. These boundary objects led women to participate in activities which gave them support.

Boundary objects facilitate connections between members of the community. Participants form close relationships with one another which originate in particular behaviour and understandings of such behaviour within the community of practice. The specialist knowledge needed to understand the workings within the community of practice prevent outsiders from entering it. The family and the extended kin offer Asian women ongoing support and mutual engagement that is distinctive, and specifically so when they enter higher education. When creating communities of practice at university, the shared references and repertoires of their communities, which outsiders did not fully understand, formed a basis on which to bond with one another. They could empathise with each other and understand why their parents wanted them to succeed and were prepared to give them the emotional and financial support they needed to do so.

8

Arranged marriages, education and changing forms of identity

Within most Asian families marriage is a means of improving and consolidating family status and its public celebration demonstrates this status. Marriage and having children are paramount concerns for parents and arranging a marriage for their children strengthens notions of community and identity for the family (Mooney, 2006). The system of arranged marriages dates back centuries and traditionally entails partners being introduced by family members. Nowadays marriage arrangers and matchmaking agencies increasingly fulfil this function. Partners tend to be matched on the basis of family reputation, wealth, caste and religion (Bhopal, 2003; Goodwin, 1999).

In many Asian societies, the main purpose of marriage is seen to be the fulfilment of community and family obligations rather than of the desires of the individual. Arranged marriages tend to be founded on concepts associated with duty rather than western ideas of falling in love. This is because the social function of the arranged marriage is to preserve group solidarity, strengthen family relationships and secure the family's economic resources within the community (Broude, 1994). The arranged marriage has been a key instrument for economic, social and political stability in Asian cultures and has been used to make political alliances, solidify economic conditions and secure social stability amongst families and communities.

Arranged marriages in India and Pakistan
Although arranged marriages are most usually seen in distinction to western traditions, there are important differences in the practices of arranged marriages within the sub-continent itself. Furthermore, the different patterns of

migration to western countries have affected marriage practices, creating variations between different destination countries and between different religious groups. Generally, Sikh and Hindu women would be expected upon marriage to move away from their families and familial village. The bride is considered a 'gift' and usually moves to her husband's home, thus isolating her from her own family. This movement has been seen as evidence of the low status of women (Jeffrey and Jeffrey, 1996). An arranged marriage of this nature might consolidate the economic and social bonds between different families. Many Muslims marriages are arranged between cousins or within the extended family network (Rao, 2000) and thus strengthen social relations within the family.

Arranged marriages in the UK

Many academic accounts support public perceptions of the arranged marriages of Asian women in the UK. They claim that the women are exploited and powerless within the marriage process, have little choice and are forced into marriage (Bhachu, 1985; Wilson, 1978). Such accounts typically compound images of strict patriarchal family structures and perpetuate an image of young Asian women as either docile, obedient and passive or as sexualised exotic 'others'. Such stereotypes have also prevailed within schools, where expectations of young girls being forced into marriage are commonplace. Parmar (1988) has argued that teachers assume that all young Asian girls will have an arranged marriage and that career aspirations are therefore unrealistic for Asian girls. Schools often assume that cultural constraints will prevent Asian girls from entering further and higher education (Brah, 1993).

Shain (2003) argued that teachers' stereotypical assumptions of Asian girls regarding marriage denied them access to the opportunities offered to other pupils. This cultural pathology interpretation of Asian culture and family life is powerful in the UK, and it is applied particularly to Muslim girls. Education is a site where relations of power and cultural definitions are constantly reinforced and challenged, and Asian girls today are actively making choices about their future careers. Contrary to dominant discourses of Asian femininity which constructs them as 'passive recipients of oppressive cultural practices', however, they are actively engaged in making choices which affect their lives (Shain, 2003:57).

A body of research in the UK has looked at the changing practices in arranged marriage in the Sikh (Ballard, 1994), Pakistani (Shaw, 2000; Werbner, 1990) and Bangladeshi communities (Gardner and Shukur, 1994). Arranged marriages amongst Asian communities in Britain do appear to have shifted away from the traditional processes described by Wilson in 1978. She explored the patriarchal nature of arranged marriages, in which women were given little choice. More recently, however, Werbner (2002) found that young people want more choice and control over choosing their marriage partner. There is evidence that many mothers who experienced arranged marriages themselves do not want to force their children into an unwanted marriage (Phillipson *et al*, 2003). The parents' social class and educational background are found to be closely linked to the degree of choice offered to children in the arrangement of marriages. 'Traditional' arranged marriages are most common amongst the least qualified and the working class (Samad and Eade, 2002). Dale *et al* (2002) identify marriage as a factor which limits the labour market prospects of some Asian women when they graduate, particularly those from Bangladeshi and Pakistani backgrounds.

Public concerns and political responses to forced marriages in the UK

In 1999 a Home Office working group was established 'to investigate the problem of forced marriage in England and Wales and to make proposals for tackling it effectively' (Home Office, 2000:10). It published *A Choice by Right*. This makes the distinction between an arranged marriage – where the family take the leading role in the selection of partner and the potential spouse has the right to say no – and a forced marriage where the individual has no choice and does not have the right to say no. But Siddiqui (2003) argues that the distinction between 'forced' and 'arranged' marriages is not clear, and is made even less clear-cut by issues such as the fears young women might have of disappointing their parents if they do not acquiesce to their marriage arrangements (Siddiqui, 2003). The option to say no might well exist, but is considered to have consequences for parents and family that would be too shocking to pursue. Accurate figures on the numbers of forced marriages in the UK are obviously hard to compile, but Werbner (2005) estimates the number at 1000 to 2000 each year.

In towns across the North of England including Bradford, Burnley and Oldham, riots erupted in 2000. In their wake came much public debate about what it means to be a British citizen, culminating in the publication of the Cantle report on *Community Cohesion* (2001). Cantle argued that Asian communities were not integrating with white British society and that consequently social cohesion was threatened. The report specifically identified areas of social policy such as housing, education and employment, in which Asian communities and white had sharply segregated interests. This sparked debate about 'Britishness' and 'citizenship' and an analysis of these concepts within media and political circles and in academia. In 2002 the then Home Secretary claimed that Asian parents should speak English to their children and marry British Asians who had grown up in the UK rather than people from the Indian sub-continent. The White Paper *Secure Borders, Safe Havens: Integration with diversity in modern Britain* (2002) gave an overview of Government thinking about migration, citizenship and the wider context of race relations in Britain. It contributed to the marking out of boundaries of exclusion and inclusion, such as who 'belongs' to the nation state and who does not, who is considered a citizen and who is not (see also Sales, 2005).

Such attitudes also informed the government's approach to 'managed migration', which attempts to distinguish between 'real' and 'bogus' migrants whilst trying to facilitate the economic benefits of controlled routes for economic migration (Lewis and Neal, 2005). Tomlinson (2005) suggests that the Cantle report also influenced the 2002 Immigration and Asylum Act, which outlined new policies for citizenship and nationality. Under this Act, all individuals who were subject to immigration control had to apply to the Home Secretary to gain 'permission' to marry. Further, the Act required future British citizens to pass an English language test. The Crick report on citizenship (2003) also emphasised that knowledge of a British language should be a prerequisite for gaining British citizenship.

The Foreign and Commonwealth Office made a policy response in their report *Community Perceptions of Forced Marriage* (Samad and Eade, 2002). This too stressed traditional practices as indicative of differences between Asian and British cultural practices. Samad and Eade (2002) argued that parents' social class and educational background are closely linked to the amount of choice children are offered in the arrangement of marriages. Parents were more likely to force their children into a marriage if they knew they were taking drugs or drinking alcohol, or if they had a partner. The report also emphasised how governmental wishes to implement policy could be easily read as racist or Islamophobic because it was concerned with sensitive issues of cultural practice.

Wilson (2006) claims that the fears flagged up by Samad and Eade about the interpretation of policy responses to cultural practices has indeed come to pass. She argues that state intervention in forced marriages has led to a huge escalation in the policing of Asian areas of Britain and that such interventions criminalise Asian communities. This has been further compounded by responses to the 'war on terror' with its criminalising of Muslim communities.

Wilson observes that *A Choice by Right* provoked racist articles in the British press about 'brutal Asian parents who were far less mature than their white counterparts and about horrendous experiences from which Asian women must be rescued' (2006:88).

In 2004, the Home Office followed growing concerns around forced marriage and honour killings, linking them to a wider initiative against 'honour crimes'. Honour killings are cases where women are killed, usually by family or community members, for crossing patriarchal boundaries and damaging family honour. These generally relate to notions of *izzat* (family pride and honour) and *sharam* (shame). Honour killings reflect the transactional aspects of traditionally arranged marriages whereby women become the property of their in-laws upon marriage. As such, their new family of in-laws act as controllers of the wife's purity and reputation. Modi (2003) asserts that honour killings are common in India amongst all religious groups, but in the UK honour killings have been associated by the media with Muslim culture (Wilson, 2006). Alongside such Western accounts of honour killings are media reports which assert, for instance, that hundreds of Asian children in school in Bradford are disappearing from school registers and expressing concern lest these children were being forced into marriages about which they had little or no choice (as in the BBC Today Programme, 2008).

Much of the research on Asian women has failed to differentiate between the diverse Asian communities and consequently fails to provide an in-depth analysis of any community. No account is taken of the marked differences of language, religion, country of origin, class, economic activity, aspirations, education levels or family size. Stereotypes constructed about Asian women are based upon cultural difference constructed in terms of fixed and immutable categories which operate to inferiorise British Asian communities. The result of much of the public debate has been to portray a stereotype in which the cultural practices of British Asians are typified most visibly by issues such as forced marriage or honour killings. This constructs Asian society as backward and alien when compared to traditional British society which is defined – also stereotypically – in terms of its civilised and progressive values. The understandings attached to such practices are used to differentiate those who belong in British society and those who do not belong (Yuval-Davis *et al*, 2005). Within the global context raised by the 'war on terror', such practices are perceived to threaten traditional British and Western values.

Women's views on arranged marriages

Asian women noted the impact of arranged marriages on their lives and stressed their strong desire to retain close links with their community and family networks, including participating in aspects of their culture, such as arranged marriages, that strengthened their belonging to their community. Familiarity with aspects of their lives which were not understood by outsiders, such as arranged marriages, was one of the strongest bonds in the communities of practice they created in university. Their familiarity and knowing was based on a shared understanding of what women's experiences might involve.

Many of the women spoke about the practice of arranged marriages and in particular discussed the changes they had noticed in the way marriages were arranged today as compared to those experienced by their parents or elder siblings and cousins. Often pointing out the greater input Asian women themselves have in the marriage process, they discussed how they identified themselves differently in relation to these practices than earlier generations of Asian women had done. But it was nonetheless a crucial difference between themselves and their non-Asian peers at university. For many of the women, there was a clear link between participating in higher education and the degree of choice they would have within the marriage process.

For Muslim women, however, there was also a clear link between their religious background and their views on arranged marriages. Marriage to first cousins is common in Pakistani origin Muslim families in Britain. Cousin marriage is thought to reduce problems with the marriage process, since familiarity and a shared kin network can help to support the couple (Charsley, 2005). Many of the Muslim women in my study told me their marriages had been or would be arranged to members of their extended families, in either the UK or Pakistan.

The impact of education

Education was seen as a means of empowerment for women. It was an opportunity to move their lives forward so that in future they would be able to participate fully in the labour market and in post-graduate studies.

> I think the best thing we can do as Asian women is to get ourselves a good education. These days you need a degree to get a job and you need a Masters degree to get a good job. For us, we need it more because we know we could be treated differently from other people because we are seen as different so we have to do really well.

Acquiring an education was related by these women to notions of self-empowerment. They saw it as giving women some control over their lives and futures and many used it as a bargaining chip for negotiating with the family and deciding who they would ultimately marry.

> I think the more education you have, the more choice and say you can have in who you will marry. That's just the way it works. You can use your education to sort of say who you do and do not want to marry. Then you don't have to marry men who are uneducated and who could hold really traditional views about life and what they want you to do with your life.

Education plays an important part in the women's lives, both personal – choosing a partner – and professional – choosing a career.

> Nowadays you have to get an education and it has to be a good education. It's just so important and if you want to get a marriage partner I think it makes a big difference because the first thing that people will ask is what sort of education have you got and what you want to do with it, or what sort of job do you do – so it does make a difference to the type of man you marry.

This was echoed by another respondent:

> I can't imagine what it would be like to leave school and then get a job without going to college or university. What kind of job would you get? Nothing more than an office job or shop work. What's the point of that? The good jobs are all very competitive now and you need a decent education to get a good job. These days everyone has got a degree and you need a degree to get a decent job. It is all very competitive so it is better to start at the right level so that you can compete with others.

Many of the women felt that certain professions – such as law, medicine and teaching – were considered respectable in Asian communities, and all required degrees. Pursuing these professions would enhance their status, in the community and their choice of marriage partner.

> I think the first thing that people ask is, what does your daughter to? What does your son do? It's the same for men and women. When my brother was going to get married, the family of the girl we thought would be a good match were keen to know this. It was the first question they asked us. So I think it can help the parents or more experienced people make their decision if they want you to meet their son or their daughter.

Educational background was seen to make a significant difference to women's lives and how they would be judged in the future. The women's backgrounds also affected how they viewed education. Those who had siblings who were or had been studying for a degree were more likely to see higher education as an asset to both the individuals and the family. Parents who were themselves educated usually wanted their daughters to be educated. Some of the women whose own parents were not from professional backgrounds nonetheless wanted their own daughters to do well at university.

In earlier research (Bhopal, 2003), I showed that women's educational background has an impact on their participation in arranged marriages. Women with first degrees and above were less likely to engage in arranged marriages and more likely to want 'love marriages'. Some were co-habiting with their partners. The women who had lower levels of education such as A-levels or below were more likely to have an arranged marriage and had less say about who they were to marry. The present research found yet a further shift in how arranged marriages are defined and the degree of power women have in negotiating the choice of marriage partner.

Dale *et al* (2002) found that educational background significantly affected the position of Pakistani and Bangladeshi women in the labour market. Women with high qualifications were more likely to be economically active than those without. Many of the women had marriages that were arranged by their parents, but with their consent after having met their prospective partners. Women with higher qualifications appeared more confident and more motivated to argue against the traditional views of marriage. Women from traditional families were more likely to get married shortly after leaving school. Like Dale *et al*'s research (2002), my research found that education was seen as the key to success and to obtaining professional status, and was related to women's positioning within the marriage market.

Social capital: managing the value of higher education

We have seen how Asian women generally engage with communities of practice. Their ability to generate useful social capital in their own lives is often tied to their engagement within communities of practice at university and the access this allows to shared knowledge and identity resources. As Balatti and Falk (2002) note, social capital is built by participation, both collective and individual, in activity that shares knowledge and identity resources. By building strong relations with other Asian women who share circumstances such as being the first family member at university, and alienated from the traditional university population, they can develop the necessary 'bridging ties' which enable active but different participation in the wider Asian community (Putnam, 1999).

Although women negotiate their identities within and outside of their community of practice, participation in higher education allows them to access appropriate networks and build levels of trust so they can share their common values. When faced with choices about participating in an arranged marriage, they can draw upon their own social capital to negotiate and change matters. In particular, social capital enables many women to secure far more favourable outcomes from cultural practices that might have disadvantaged them in the past, such as arranged marriages. Within the dynamic relations between individuals, communities of practice, family and wider communities, Asian women are using higher education to build their social capital in the wider world.

Wenger (1998) argues that learning events in communities of practice are integrated into the formation of identities. This was apparent in many of the women's lives, as they negotiated new senses of belonging within their university networks. This process creates ongoing shared histories in which new accounts of identity are generated as the women come to understand how their lives differ from those of earlier generations. Their participation within local communities of practice has a direct relationship with the wider relationships to communities outside the university. These different relationships inevitably have a mutual impact: so for example Asian women might share and adapt to the novelty of attending university by creating strategies to support themselves in an alien environment.

Whilst such endeavours work mostly within local spaces, Asian women also deal with global concerns, for example learning to position themselves in relation to public debate about 'forced marriages', 'honour killings' or 'the war on terror'. Using communities of practice allows them to transfer their readily accessible local knowledge such as shared experiences of higher education to wider settings such as their marriage and future employment prospects. This is the great strength of communities of practice. It is all the more remarkable because it works even when there is hostility from traditionalist Asian culture or from fallout of 'the war on terror'. Wenger (1998) rightly argues that the relationship between the local and global are related to levels of participation and these always coexist and shape each other.

Shared communities of belonging – women's views on arranged marriages

Being a member of a community of practice gave the women a shared understanding. Part of this was based on their commonality of experience concerning the cultural experiences of engaging in an arranged marriage; part was based on their participation in higher education and the notions of self-empowerment this engendered and the possibility of having some control over their future.

Some of the women told me that their cultural background might require them to have an arranged marriage, whereas others said that marriages were no longer arranged in the way they used to be, but that they would respond to introductions to suitors. A minority of women from all three religious backgrounds said their parents might not necessarily want them to have an arranged marriage.

> In my extended family, some of my distant relatives – the girls – all got married when they were really young and they had strict arranged marriages. They didn't go to university, so they had less of a say in how the marriage went. For many of us now and for me and my sisters, we have more choices because we're being educated and then we can say to our parents that we want to marry a boy who is the same as us and who has the same sort of education as us. But if you haven't got the education yourself, how can you ask other people to have it?

Another respondent explicitly saw education as a means of enabling women to have more power and control over the marriage process.

> I just think it makes you have more say in the way your life goes and what you want to do with it and who you want to ultimately marry. And that can be a powerful thing and can make the difference to how your life will turn out.

Many women felt that obtaining a degree was very important, not only for themselves but also for their parents, who recognised the impact it might have on their daughter's future choices. One said:

> For me, I see it as just the beginning, because I want to make sure I do more than this. I want to have a good future and security. I want to do a Masters and maybe more after this – it means a lot to me and I know it means a lot to my parents. They want me to do well and they have invested a lot in it – money, time and the support they give me. So I want to do well, for me and for my family.

Parental pressure was seen as an important impetus for study. Some women felt that although their parents wanted them to do well, they might not be comfortable about the fact that higher education would give them greater power in negotiating their marriage.

I think it can be hard for our parents. Because they want us to do well, they want us to get educated because they know that's the best thing for us. But at the same time, they know that once we get educated we don't want the traditional arranged marriage that they may have had. Times have changed and we want more now. Asian women want more and they want more control and influence over their life. I think you have to change to move on and it's inevitable. We have to change with the times and our parents know that.

These days marriage has changed in the Asian community. It's not as strict as it once used to be and it's based more now on what the young people want. Parents are ok with that because they know that their children will do what they want anyway. That's one of the reasons that I think parents encourage their children to go to university so that their children can have a better life.

Many of the women in the study felt that arranged marriages no longer existed as such. Some of the Muslim women mentioned the tradition of marrying first cousins, but emphasised that they had a choice in this.

In some Muslim cultures you can marry your cousin and that is usually a decision that is made when you are very young. And for some reasons this can work, but these days families are moving away from this kind of arrangement.

Some Muslim women did report that their marriage partners had already been chosen for them from an early age. Some of the men were in the UK and some in Pakistan.

I think we are more strict than say Hindu or Sikh communities when it comes to marriage. Often when we are very young our parents choose who we are going to marry and that's because we have a tradition of marrying our first cousins and so it's easy for our parents to find someone for us to marry. My parents have told me that I will be marrying my first cousin and I have to go with that. I can't see them changing and saying I could marry someone else. It is something that was agreed a long time ago.

Another Muslim respondent acknowledged the practice of such arranged marriages but felt resentful about having to go back to Pakistan and marry her first cousin.

I know that I will have to go back home to get married. My parents have let me do a degree because I am still living at home and they said I was lucky because I could have been married a long time ago. My parents want me to go back to Pakistan to get married and I know that this was something that was agreed a long time. That doesn't mean that I don't want it. If I have my own choice I would rather marry a boy from here.

Some of the Muslim women resisted and delayed marriage, but knew that it would happen eventually.

> I could have been married a long time ago, but I managed to get my parents to let me go to university and they agreed. I think they do see the value of education, but they also see the value of the community and know what it means to them. They do want us to be married eventually, so we have to listen to them as well. To them, if they let us study then they see that as encouraging us to do well in our life, but they also see the importance of us having to get married in the community.

Many of the Hindu women felt that marriages were now arranged in a different way. They saw arranging as an 'introduction' and believed they would have more choice, rather than being told whom they were to marry.

> I don't think that arranged marriages exist as such as any more to tell you the truth. But then it depends on the family. In my family, because we are all at university we know that our parents do want us to get married but they go about it in a different way now. I know when my parents were married it was a proper arranged marriage, for us it's more of an introduction.

This respondent described how the process of choosing a life partner worked.

> Someone in the family will tell my parents that there's this guy and my parents will find out as much as they can about him and his family. But he needs to be from the right kind of family, he will have to have a good education, speak well and really have some money as well. That is important in our culture – if you have money and are educated you have a lot of status. Money and education on their own do give you status on their own, but it's better to have both. If he fits the bill, then my parents will speak to his parents or someone who knows the family and me and him will get to meet. If we like each other we can start to go out and the difference now is that we can actually say no or say we don't want to meet him. In the past some girls were not allowed to meet the boy or go out with him, now the marriages are not so traditional and are very modern. You have more choice and you have more say.

This new system of arranged marriages seemed to work better than the old because it suited the needs of both the parents and their children. Many of the women said that ultimately parents wanted their children to have marriages that were arranged so their daughters could marry men who were 'like them'. One of the Sikh women said:

> At the end of the day, our parents want us to stay in the culture, it's one thing that they know is important to us and so they want to keep it as much as they

can. And yet at the same time, they know the culture has to change somewhat so that means they allow us to have more freedom in our lives and they allow us to have the choice when it comes to choosing a husband for us.

On the one hand, the culture and identity of what it meant to be an Asian woman in British society was strongly preserved, but on the other hand it was recognised that some change was inevitable and that women should have more freedom and greater choice in their lives. Another Sikh woman told me:

My oldest sister was not allowed to leave home to go to university, she had to go to the local university, but with me things were different. My parents accepted that everyone my age was going away to study and they had to allow me to do that. Times have changed and I think people have to change with them.

The impact of education on determining marriage partners

Level of education and parental background strongly influenced who parents introduced their daughters to. If a prospective spouse fitted the initial criteria, the parents would decide whether they wanted their daughter to meet him.

Many of the women spoke about *izzat*. *Izzat* is based on family honour and pride and is usually controlled by the senior members of the family. In some communities it is used to keep women powerless within the family. This creates great pressure on women to obey strict moral codes and to conform to suitable notions of 'femininity'. Many of the Hindu and Sikh women emphasised that *izzat* was not as important as it once was.

My mum speaks about *izzat* and does refer to it and says how important it is. I sort of know what she means because you don't want people to say bad things about your family and about your daughters. So we all have to behave properly. But then I don't think it's as important as it used to be, because people have changed and times have changed as well.

Izzat and its controlling effects were related to religion and parental background. The Muslim respondents spoke about its importance and its effect on the family.

We do have to think about how we are seen in the family and how the community sees us. So, of course it is important for my family to monitor the way I dress and the way I behave in public. I know there are things I can and cannot do and I have to abide by those rules.

I would say *izzat* is important, it is more important if you're a girl. It's about respect and not doing things that would embarrass your parents. As Muslims your standing in the community is important – more so if you are female. If you step out of line, everyone will know about it and they will talk about it and it is your parents who people will say things to. It depends on how strict your parents are as well.

Many of the Muslim women in the study indicated that religion would continue to play an important part in their lives whether or not they went to university. Equally, they did not doubt that their parents would want them to marry a Muslim.

For us it's different, being Muslim. It depends on how religious you are and how religious your parents are. My parents are quite religious and they want us to continue with religion as they see it as being important. But at the same time they want us to get a good education. You can have both at the same time, they are not exclusive. My parents have said we can have a choice in who we marry. They would prefer it was a Muslim with a good education.

Whilst some Hindu and Sikh women noted a shift in the desirable qualities their parents ascribed to a marriage partner that might privilege his educational background rather than his religion, this was rarely the case for Muslim women. A Muslim respondent explained the greater emphasis on religious background:

I think my parents would say that religion is more important to them than the education. Because the religion is the way of life, it's what you do everyday and so you have to have someone who understands that. If I did meet someone who was Muslim they would be happy with that. If he wasn't Muslim my parents would want him to think about converting. That's how important our religion is to us in our family.

For many Muslim women, attending university required a greater degree of negotiation with their parents about their standing in the community so they could reassure them about how they would cope with exposure to non-Muslim culture. Some of the women said one reason their parents allowed them to attend university was because it was local and they would be with other Muslim girls. This suggested that traditional notions of honour would be maintained because of the shared awareness of what was acceptable behaviour for Muslim girls. The pressure about acceptable behaviour was felt to extend as far as a local university.

My parents are quite strict Muslims and I had to fight to get to university, but when they thought about it and they knew it was only a bus ride away and that there were lots of other Asian Muslim women at the university they were ok with it. They now realise that it was the best thing for me. Because they know that it will make a difference to my life and what I decide to do.

This young woman also talked about shame or *sharam*. This too was related control of women and to how their behaviour affected how the family was seen in the community. Women's behaviour was closely monitored. A woman who brought shame upon the family jeopardised the family's reputation. Muslim women emphasised the importance of shame, but overall many of the women indicated that the power of *sharam* was declining.

We still do think of what we do and we know that doing certain things would bring shame on the family and you would be blamed for that. So we know what we can and can't do. But then again *sharam* isn't as bad as it used to be. The community would be watching out for you and seeing how you would behave so that they would go and tell their parents and you would be told off. That doesn't seem to happen too much now. The whole community has moved on and people have modern attitudes now and they see that *sharam* and what people think doesn't matter as much as their children being happy. Parents want their children to be happy, they don't want them to run away and not have contact with them. This used to happen a lot, you would hear stories about girls having to run away because their parents would not accept that they had a boy-friend.

Hindu and Sikh respondents placed less emphasis on the importance of *sharam* than the Muslim women did.

I think that these days, families are more independent they care more about their children than what the community thinks. They want their children to be happy and another reason is because parents know we are independent so they have to listen to us rather than the community because we could say to them that we are leaving home. They don't want us to do that so they talk to us more and we discuss things.

Many of the women observed that women they knew who came from backgrounds with little or no education were more concerned about *izzat* and *sharam* and that these controls were more likely to affect them. They saw these women as having little bargaining power over their marriages: they had less choice about who they would marry and less control over their own lives. A background in which they were encouraged to achieve high levels of education gave women greater power and choice of husband. They were able to use their education as a bargaining resource.

The westernisation of marriage

Many of the women commented that the way marriages were arranged now reflected aspects of western marriage. Whilst this did not mean that Asian families were opting for traditional British white weddings, they followed certain customs such as cutting the wedding cake, wearing a white wedding dress, the bride and groom leading the first dance of the evening, going on honeymoon and even having a wedding list. Not only had the processes involved in the selection of partners shifted but so too had wedding practices. The women told me that this was at the request of the bride and groom rather than of the parents or extended family.

For women in particular, increased participation rates in education and employment had a direct impact on their right to influence the actual wedding day. Many of the respondents said that changes in the wedding procedure was more to do with what the bride and groom wanted, overriding the parents' wishes.

> It is about keeping the bride and groom happy. They are the ones who want to do all these modern things, it's not the parents, they would be quite happy to go along with the ordinary traditional things that they are used to. When my brother got married it was his wife – more than him – but him as well who wanted to cut a cake and wear a white wedding dress and go on a honeymoon. My parents did it because they wanted them to be happy. It could also be that the parents may think if they don't do what the bride and groom ask then the couple may go off and get married by themselves – which they would not want.

> The whole wedding thing these days has changed so much. Much more than when our mothers or even our older sisters got married. These days they have white wedding cakes, wedding dresses and all sorts. To me it's like they [Asian people] want the weddings to be the same as English weddings and so they do the same things that traditional British people do at their weddings. It's also related to the fact that a lot of marriages are not really arranged any more like they used to be. The wedding day is such a big thing for the families, so it's usually the girl who wants all these extra things like the cake and the dress, because it's her day – so she can have what she wants. Most parents are ok with it and think it's a good idea.

Respondents related the change in arranged marriages to changing notions of Asian and *British Asian* identity. These changes were emphasised more by the Hindu and Sikh respondents:

> Who would have thought that we would have things like the bride and groom having the first dance and the bride would be wearing a white dress with a tiara!

> And then they go off on honeymoon. It's all modernised so much and has changed completely. It was bound to really because we have changed from being here [in England] for such a long time. Lots of Asian people now want to assert their British identity as much as they want to assert their Asian identity. But they want to pick and choose what that is and so in the marriage they choose to do a lot of things the western way and at the same time they still choose to do things the Asian way – so you could say they mix and match. They have weddings which cater for both parts – the Asian part and the British part – I suppose it's to satisfy us, because we see ourselves as being both.

Muslim women, however, were more likely to emphasise the traditional aspects of marriages.

> We don't tend to have the more modern marriages like discos and things, ours are more traditional and that may be because we emphasise religion more and other Asian families do not.

Overall, the women could negotiate their own definitions of femininity and what this means in relation to the marriage process. They could question the traditional form of marriage and what this means for their feminine identity. This has led to a reassessment of women's identity in relation to the changing gendered and racialised discourses around identity and selfhood. They are not 'caught between two cultures' but can rather pick and choose various aspects of British and Asian culture to form new identities in British Asian society. For some, this may include redefining the practice of arranged marriage; for others it may mean opting out of marriage completely. Either way, women have greater choice in the decisions they make regarding marriage and the family. One Sikh woman described how...

> as a woman I have greater control over my life and my parents understand that now. I am an adult but I also have respect for my parents and the culture. But if I said to them I wanted to go on a honeymoon and have a wedding cake and a disco when I get married – which I probably will – they will be ok with that. These things are not Asian, they are more British, but we can take the things we like and adapt those for us when we get married. People are changing who they are all the time, I think that change will be more apparent as time goes on.

Asian women today have a range of diverse identities they can choose from and can adapt changes within both British society and Asian communities to suit their identity.

> We do have more choice now and that choice is seen in lots of different ways. It starts off with we have more choice in who we marry – with the help of our

parents – but they won't force us to marry someone we don't want to marry. We have more choice now because times have changed and because our parents want us to be happy. They are less concerned about what people outside of the family think. That's why when I get married if I want to have a honeymoon or a cake – things that aren't really traditional to our Asian weddings then I will have those things – and my parents will understand that.

The changing identities of Asian women reflect Wenger's (1998) notion of identities forming trajectories both *within* and *across* communities of practice. Identity is an ongoing process which is based on the interaction of divergent trajectories. Women's participation in higher education links their boundary trajectories with those of the family and the wider world. Asian women are involved in what Wenger describes as 'brokering work' (1998:154), in which they make connections between their communities of practice and their lives as students, and their families and community.

Brokering allows the women to make connections across different communities of practice and these can open up new possibilities about the meanings they give to different events. So whilst attending university might in the past have been a questionable activity that threatened many traditional expectations of the role of Asian women, now it is realigned within new meanings of what it means to be a successful Asian woman, both as an individual and within the family community. According to Wenger, 'a sense of trajectory gives us ways of sorting out what matters and what does not, what constitutes our identity and what remains marginal' (1998:155).

For Asian women, being on an educational trajectory provides different perspectives on their participation and identities in higher education and within their traditional communities. Their continuing engagement in their family and community life shapes the trajectories they construct for themselves. Whilst their past identities may have been similar to those of their mothers, their present and future selves are determined by how they negotiate and change their identities when facing challenges their mothers never faced. The greatest impact of attending university and engaging in new communities of practice in higher education is the generation of cultural shifts, such as vastly increased choice over who they will marry and the terms of the marriage itself.

Conclusions

The one constant in the lives of Asian women living in Britain is that they are above all in a period of significant ongoing change. What is more, this change is universal; it affects not just Asian women but all Asian people and communities in Britain. The realignments of the various Asian communities need to be seen also in relation to white British society and to life on the Indian sub-continent. In Britain we are seeing the shift from being newly arrived as migrants with no base or roots in an alien country, to being part of one of the well-established communities whose children and grandchildren were born in Britain. We see confident communities who have built their own social and religious structures and have become engaged in the political and social landscape of the British 'other'.

Although the over-arching change for Asian communities might indicate an integrationist approach to life in Britain, this is not quite so. Rather, what is emerging is a new set of identities that manage both the pressures of being part of a migrant culture and the challenges of shaping culture of a different kind. This is perhaps most visible in the case of Asian women, because the earlier expectations for Asian women diverged so greatly from those of white British women. Young Asian women had most to gain in terms of personal liberation from traditional and patriarchal structures – more even than their brothers. The space allowed for them to re-think their identity has been within higher education, partly because their economic capital multiplies once they have a degree. But while at university, they develop support networks with Asian women from similar backgrounds and these networks provide a social space in which they can together rethink their identities. That the impact of this change is seen so clearly with Asian women is because it generates new types of identities, not just in the spaces of the university or later at the workplace but, more importantly, also within the traditional Asian communities in the UK. The economic potential of higher education is translated into greater personal freedom and independence in the home and this is particularly apparent with regard to marriage. This new identity formation is no longer based on an assumption that the husband will be the main breadwinner and his wife will remain at home since this no longer makes practical or economic sense.

Many women described their identities as *British Asian*. Marking this difference between themselves and other British women signals the particular way many Asian women position themselves. One side of their identity is marked by the distinction between their lives and that of their mothers, and the realignment of their roles within traditional family and community life. The other side of their identity is characterised by the gulf between the lives of Asian women and white women.

In their new identities, British Asian women seek to reconcile and maintain aspects of their traditional culture because they still value it. When choosing new paths for their future careers that are financially advantageous, the women are clearly following a route that their families support. Like them, their parents want them to go to university, succeed in their studies and pursue well paid careers; moreover, they recognise that doing so will disrupt traditional practices such as arranged marriages. Between parents and daughters is a new willingness to take practical measures that will improve their future stability and affluence. They also share a new approach to arranged marriages that acknowledges the greater role their daughters desire in choosing their husband. The arranged marriage retains many of its traditional functions of social and economic bonding between families and within the community, but does so in recognition of women's economic role and allowing them greater individual choice. The changing approach to marriage protects the individual interests of Asian women but also retains important elements of their cultural heritage. The importance placed on family life remains at the centre of these new identities.

9

Dowries: past, present and future

Dowries are an aspect of arranged marriages. The uncomfortable notion of exchanging a bride for cash or other goods positions women as trading counters within Asian society. We have seen how important weddings are for Asian households in both the Indian sub-continent and the UK, marking an event in the familial cycle, as new alliances are created and existing ones strengthened. Marriage partners are generally assessed according to their education, employment, wealth and social class as well their as caste membership. In both India and the UK, dowries have been a traditional feature of arranged marriages for centuries.

Traditionally, the bride's family makes payments to the groom and his family at the time of the marriage. In the past, dowry gifts were small tokens of good wishes for the couple on their wedding day. More recently however, the dowry has become a substantial transfer of wealth from the bride's family to the groom's and is a major factor in marriage negotiations (Srinivasan and Lee, 2004). Different hierarchies exist between 'wife givers' and 'wife receivers' and these are highlighted by the hospitality and gifts that are given to the groom and his family. The custom has been observed by anthropologists such as Charsley (2005) and sociologists such as Wilson (1978). Change and continuity have been examined within the context of migration through rituals such as the dowry (Ballard, 1978; Bhachu, 1985).

Women's university attendance has affected dowry practice within the UK. In the past it was assumed that women would not contribute to the economy of the family (Boserup, 1970) and the dowry was seen as a way of compensating the groom and his family for the economic support they would provide for the bride. The women's role in her future in-laws' family would primarily be as a homemaker. Today, the assumption is that a highly educated woman will pursue a well paid career after university. In the past dowries were agreed in relation to, among other matters the cost of the wedding celebrations, the gifts given to the bride and groom from the bride's family or the gifts the bride took with her to her husband's house and in this sense could be seen to represent the woman's inheritance (Menski, 1998). Sharma (1984), however, argues that the dowry does not represent a fixed share of the bride's inheritance but rather is the outcome of marriage negotiations; alternatively, dowry could be in the form of property or cash demanded of the bride by the groom's family (Srinivas, 1984).

In India, dowry exists for all religions and all classes (Mandelbaum, 1999; Stone and James, 1995). The practice reflects the inferior position of women in India, where preference is always for male children. Female mortality in some parts of India such as the Punjab is higher at all ages than male mortality, which Das Gupta (1987) explained as due to boys receiving better medical care than girls. Sons are preferred in India, causing the abortion of more female foetuses as well as infanticide of girl babies (Das Gupta, 1987; Srinivasan and Lee, 2004). The practice of dowries is reinforced by the patriarchal practices which keep women in India in an inferior position (Walton-Roberts, 2004).

Jhutti (1998) examined escalating dowry demands amongst some Asian communities in Britain and found that gifts of furniture and other household goods given to the groom on marriage can even remain in the groom's home if the couple move out. In other cases, the bride's parents may furnish the groom's home in place of the dowry, though money may also be given.

The advantages of dowry practice

The size of the dowry is seen as one way for the bride's family to become socially mobile if it enhances their social status by attracting a groom of higher status than they are; at the same time the groom's family are able to select the most economically desirable bride from a large pool of eligible brides (Kumari, 1989). As the dowry is symbolic of the social and economic position of the bride's family, providing a large and ostentatious dowry increases their own status. A more than generous dowry can also be seen as a way of ensuring that daughters are treated well after marriage and shown favourable treatment in the marital home, such as giving her less household tasks and greater autonomy (Sharma, 1984). The parents of the bride are expected to keep giving the groom and his family gifts on social occasions or family gatherings.

According to McCoid (1989), the dowry is seen as an easy route to greater wealth and upward social mobility. Marriage and dowries are crucial in maintaining family ties and kinship obligations, and thus can influence migration (Walton-Roberts, 2003). The process of finding a suitable marriage partner and arranging marriages in which dowries are exchanged fosters notions of collectivity and expresses the notion of community boundaries in which respectability and honour are crucial for the maintenance of a stable family and extended kin relationships.

Prasad (1994) argued that women are supportive of the dowry principle as they play a role in negotiating a dowry for their sons, and daughters may place value on the monetary and material wealth that is transferred from their parents to their in-laws (Krishanaswamy, 1995). Young couples see the dowry as a way in which to access material resources, indicating the increasing desirability of consumer goods (Matthew, 1987).

The disadvantages of dowry practice

Notwithstanding women's increasing participation in the labour market, dowry practice persists (see Srinivasan and Lee, 2004). The expense associated with the marriage of a daughter and the dowry can be financially crippling for parents (Bhat and Halli, 1999). As a consequence they view daughters as a financial burden which demands extreme financial investment with little return.

The frequency of violence against wives who bring too little a dowry is a growing problem in India (Stone and James, 1995). Kumar (2003) reports that the bride can be subjected to abuse from her in-laws if dowry demands are not met and this can entail mental and physical harassment to encourage the family to fulfil dowry obligations that exist before, during and after the marriage. Sons are perceived as having economic, social and religious value while daughters are often an economic liability because of the dowry system. Researchers such as Edlund (2006) have argued that the practice of dowry indicates that dowry is the price women pay for marriage.

According to Oldenburg (2002), dowries in northern India until the mid-nineteenth century were the property of women, given to them at marriage. By the early twentieth century the practice of dowry had changed from belonging to the bride to a public display of gifts to everyone who attended the wedding. Control of the dowry shifted from the bride to her husband and in-laws. The public display of dowry to all the family and community has caused it to become hugely competitive, putting parents under pressure to provide ever more expensive dowries (Wilson, 2006).

Changes in dowry practice

Arguably, modernisation and social change cause traditional Asian practices such as dowries and arranged marriages gradually to disappear (Teja, 1991). However, the Asian dowry system and the practice of arranged marriages have been resistant to social change in India. Matthew (1987) asserts that the younger generation hold more favourable attitudes towards dowries than their parents. Krishnaswamy (1995) claims that those from high status backgrounds favour dowries more than those from lower status backgrounds. However, Sirnvasan and Lee (2004) have argued that highly educated young women who are exposed to modern influences through the media are less likely to support the tradition. Employed women are likely to be exposed to liberal views in the workplace and their greater financial independence encourages them to question traditional practices which they feel might burden their parents (Malhotra and Mathar, 1997). But women who only contribute unpaid work to the family enterprise are likely to support the dowry, as they value the resources dowries bring. So if women move out of unpaid employment in the family to paid employment in the labour market then support for the dowry might diminish (Srinivasan and Lee, 2004). However, dowries are still often regarded as important components of a marriage system that itself may be changing too rapidly, as culture becomes more materialistic (Paul, 1985; Teja, 1991). There is evidence that decreased fertility among higher status families increases the competition for desirable husbands and as this competition is economic, dowries may be regarded as necessary, even if undesirable (Srinvasan and Lee, 2004).

Sikhs, Hindus and dowries

For many Sikhs and Hindus potential marriage matches and the giving of dowries is assessed by the educational and employment achievements of the couple and the wider family, as well as by wealth and the possibility for it to increase. Mooney (2006) claims that in Sikh and Hindu families, dowries and marriage are related to the position of women in Asian communities,

> ...cultural practices around Punjabi marriage are what most reflect the inferior social position of women in both Sikh and Hindu communities: dowry, hypergamous marriage and patrilocal residence constitute women as subordinate, disempower them from rights over property and remove them from their comparative security of their natal homes. (2006:396)

The grooms' families can demand cars, cash and gold in addition to the traditional gifts of clothing and jewellery, which constitute the bride's moveable inheritance (Goody, 1993). In this system, Sikh and Hindu women are disadvantaged also when their association with their birth family is weakened at marriage by the separation of the bride from her family, both physically and emotionally. Singh and Tatla (2006) report dowry demands in some Sikh marriages in the UK, have increased, with some parents of the groom demanding excessive gifts such as a house or sports car. As the participation of young people in the labour market increases, the bride and groom are more likely to pay for or contribute to their wedding and to the dowry.

Muslims and dowries

Generally speaking, dowry giving is not a custom of Islam, although it is on the increase in Muslim cultures originating in India and Bangladesh (*Islam for Today*, 2008). However, the *mahr* in Pakistan is a compulsory part of the Islamic marriage contract. This is a gift of money, possessions or property made by the husband to the wife, which becomes her exclusive property at marriage. It is an admission of her independence, enabling her to start her marriage with money or property that she can claim as her own. Shaw (2000) found an increase over time in the numbers of first cousin marriages amongst British Pakistanis. As we saw, such marriages are considered advantageous as they strengthen kin and family ties (Donnan, 1988). Kin will be able to assess the compatibility of partners and if there are problems in the marriage a shared network of kin would prove supportive (Fischer and Lyon, 2000). Kin marriage can be a source of refuge and support for women (Kapadia, 1995).

Women who marry their first cousins are more likely to support the dowry as the groom's parents will probably not make excessive demands on their own relatives. Thus, the dowry is more for the benefit of the couple than the groom's parents and his family (Reddy, 1988).

Transnational migration, dowries and marriage

Writers in the UK have examined the concept of transnational migration in relation to family life (eg Ballard, 1994) and note the important role of women in community formation and the maintenance of social networks in the process of migration (Werbner, 1990; 1996). Mooney (2006) states that transnational marriage removes the requirement for dowry for the bride and groom. For British Pakistanis involved in transnational marriages, gifts of furniture and household goods may be given to the couple even if they leave them behind in the groom's parental home and settle in Britain. Or the bride's parents might equip the couple's home instead of paying a dowry (Charsley, 2003). Walton-Roberts (2004) claims that in the process of transnational marriage, the woman's educational background is important when finding a match, but that it has not reduced the expectation of dowry. Global consumerism has had an effect on the practice of dowries and it is women who are considered the most vulnerable subjects in the reproduction of traditional gendered hierarchies. Dominant ideologies of masculine and feminine behaviour reflect the contributions of families to dowries and their status within Asian communities.

Dowry practice and women in higher education

I asked my respondents about the giving of dowries and whether or not their increased participation in higher education and the labour market affected the practice. Although there are cultural differences in the giving of dowries, all the women told me that the practice of dowries had changed significantly in the last ten years. It was the Sikh and Hindu women who talked more about the tradition of dowry practice in their communities.

> Dowries did exist in the proper sense a long time ago, maybe ten years ago. But now I think the situation is changing a lot. People have changed and times have changed. More women are getting educated and they want to pay for their own marriages now with their husbands. The parents do contribute, but it's like giving presents, which happens in all cultures.

Others said that dowries were seen as presents nowadays. Overt examples of the commodification of women, such as prospective in-laws demanding large dowries, were largely a thing of the past. As one Sikh woman said:

> It used to be that dowries were used to sell women. There was a lot of pressure on parents to give a big dowry and they had to do that. It was as if the groom and his family had a lot of power. It may still be like that in India and in some cultures here, but for me and the people I know it's changed a lot.

Another respondent observed that despite parents wanting to give large dowries because they felt this was part of their cultural tradition, there was greater pressure from within their families to change dowry practice. In particular, the potential independence of educated daughters entering the job market dramatically changed how dowries might be negotiated, with the daughters themselves assuming a powerful position.

> For many parents they just had to continue to give the dowries because they saw it as a practice that they had to continue and could not stop. There was a lot of pressure on parents and now things are different. Parents know that they have to change otherwise they may lose their daughters, because lots of women are getting a good education and that means they will have more say in what

they can do in their lives. So then parents listen to them because they know deep down that if they don't then the women will leave and do their own thing.

Many of the women noted aspects of the westernisation of marriage, including a reassessment of the meaning of dowry giving. Dowries were talked about as being just presents given on the wedding day, just as presents were given to people in other cultures on their wedding day.

Other people give presents on their wedding day and that's what we do. We do the same as what other people do. If you look at English cultures, the father of the bride pays for the wedding and people don't question that. But when they look at Asian cultures that's kind of what we do and people just interpret it differently. But that's because they use their western way of defining it and it's sort of not right for people to do that.

This quote captures the ambiguity that is apparent when modern young Asian women discuss dowries. Although she herself suggests that British people giving wedding presents is comparable to dowry practice, she sees this as a western interpretation. It seems that the traditional Asian role of dowry and the linkage between dowry and an inferior status for women in Asian cultures is still understood, even if only as a throwback to traditional roots, not as modern day practice. Some of this ambiguity also emerged when I asked the women directly whether they thought dowries were oppressive to women. Many disagreed and were offended by this suggestion but they all agreed that dowries might have been oppressive in the past.

It's not oppressive because it's part of the culture and when people did do it, it was seen as part of the way in which people did things back then and now it has changed. I think to say it is oppressive is based on the interpretation of it.

It's not oppressive, it was in the past and was much more about the display of money and how much you had. These days it's more about what the parents can provide for their children when they start their married life. A lot of the times now, the couple pay for things as well and a lot of the times the marriages aren't strictly arranged anyway.

I think that there used to be a lot of pressure on parents to provide a large dowry and they had no choice in this. Some people felt they had to do it otherwise the community would judge them and they would look bad. It has changed a lot now. People know that everyone can't afford to give a large dowry and some parents have to work hard for years to save for it. It shouldn't be so much pressure for people because parents should be allowed to give what they can for their daughters.

The women appeared to regard dowry practice as having been an oppressive practice in the past, but that it could be understood within the terms of traditional Asian culture. They resented non-Asians making judgements about how their culture had organised itself in the past. This seemed slightly disingenuous, making me suspect that some of the criticisms of dowry practice voiced within their social networks on campus would be considered unacceptable if made by a white, middle class lecturer. When asked whether dowries were used to sell women for marriage, many disagreed but nevertheless acknowledged that this might once have been the case:

> I think that's not true at all. That sounds a bit extreme to me. Maybe it was like that a long time ago and maybe it's like that back home in India in the poorer places and the villages. I don't think people see it like that – not here and not with the people I know.

Many respondents felt things had changed:

> It depends on how you look at it. For some women, it might be seen like this – maybe those who have no choice and say in who they will marry and so their parents have to find the person for them and they might not have any education, so that means they won't have any choice. But for me and the people I know, it's not like that at all.

> It depends how much you want your daughter to get married. If there is a lot of pressure from the community to make sure that your daughters are married off, then there is a lot of pressure to give a big dowry. Those parents who succumb to that pressure are the ones who may feel they have no choice and can't get any better.

The women believed that as society was changing so too were the Asian traditional practices. As more women are entering higher education and consequently have greater financial and economic independence in the labour market, they have more influence over the dowry process.

Most of the Muslim respondents distinguished clearly between the dowry practices of Sikh and Hindu families, and the Muslim practice of *mahr*, the gifts given to the bride by the groom.

> Our system of dowries is different because it is more religious based. It is the husband who has to give something to the wife so that she starts the marriage with her own money. This is an old tradition, but I think it only exists when the families are very religious.

However, many of the Muslim women also spoke about how the tradition of giving dowries had increased in the UK.

> Dowries are given in Muslim communities now but that's with those who are not so strict. If they are strict Muslims then they give the *mahr*, which is something that some people do.

> I know that some Muslim people do have dowries now like the Hindus and the Sikhs. It's very similar but not as rigid as people think. The bride's family does have to pay for a lot but the groom's family and both the couple pay for a lot of things as well.

Research corroborates these comments. The dowry practice she describes, however, is based on contributions from both families rather than solely from the bride and her family.

Who pays?

Asked what happens with dowries in practice – who gives what to whom – the women were clear that the actual practice of dowries had changed too. Many said that parents in the past had full control over the dowry, that the money for the dowry came from the parents and they decided how it was spent. But nowadays women's greater earning power gave them more say in who paid for what. A Sikh woman said:

> The dowry has changed now – it's not really a dowry as such. Before it was the parents who made all the decisions about it, but now the decision is more of a joint decision made with the bride and also her future husband. When my sister was married last year my parents paid for most of the things and because she was working and she had been working for a few years, so she was also able to pay for some things. She didn't mind and she just saw it as something that would help my parents and also she knew the things she was paying for were for her and her husband and her future in-laws.

Being able to contribute to the costs of the dowry also gave women greater say in how it was spent. A Hindu woman said:

> Because you pay for a lot of things yourself when it comes to the gifts you have to buy this means you can choose what you want. My cousins chose their own clothes and furniture that they were going to have when they got married. They also chose their own gold, which they wear at the wedding. They also did this with their husbands to be – they chose things together because they were both paying for it. This didn't seem to happen so much in the past, the parents did it all. That doesn't happen so much nowadays.

Parents were more likely to pay for the actual wedding day, much like the traditional practice in non-Asian cultures.

> Parents do pay for a lot. They pay for the whole of the wedding day, which can be very expensive, and they want to pay because they are your parents. But it does all amount to a lot because a lot of Asian weddings last several days and can go on and you have to pay for all those things.

> These days it's all about everyone making a contribution to the wedding – from the parents – and the grooms' parents also contribute now. The bride and the groom and both of their families pay for it all. It's better that way because it means there's less stress on the families and they don't have to think they have to work hard to pay for a very big expensive wedding themselves and the gifts that come with the wedding. There is less stress for them if they know their children will also help out.

Participation in the labour market directly determined whether the bride and groom were able to contribute to the dowry and the wedding.

> If the daughter is not working of course she can't contribute to the wedding if she doesn't have any money. But these days' most Asian women are working and they know that one day they will get married and so they are happy for their money to be used in this way – it is for their future. If they are not working this is unusual, that's also one of the reasons why a lot of Asian women want to get their degrees so that they can get a good job and become independent.

Many of the women spoke about how economic independence affected what they were able to do after they were married. In the past, couples were expected to live with their in-laws after marriage and the groom's brother and his family might have lived in the same household with their parents. In some cases, this caused conflict and many women did not find the situation ideal. However, there has been a shift away from this practice among all three faith groups (Singh and Tatla, 2006; Wilson, 2006), as I was told:

> If you are working and you are paying for the wedding and all the presents, then a lot of people nowadays have a lot of money that they can save. When they live with their parents they don't have to pay any rent or pay for food and so you can save all your money. This money is then used to pay for the wedding and all the gifts that come with it. Some people also use the money for a deposit on a house so that they don't have to move in with their in-laws, which has always been the tradition in Asian families. That doesn't happen so much now.

> Lots of people now – especially women – when they get married they don't want to start their married life with their in-laws do they? Instead they want to

have their own houses rather than having to live with their in-laws and their family. Sometimes they have to live with the brother and all of his family as well. These days though a lot of families are moving away from this tradition and because women work and contribute financially they can have more say in what they want to do after they are married and where they want to live. You also find that the groom wants to do this as well, they don't want to live with their parents anymore. That is now considered old fashioned and times have moved on from this. Some people might live with the family and in-laws when they are first married, because it's the tradition, but only for a short while. Then after a few months they might move out into their own place.

Clearly, the source of money associated with dowries had changed, with more of it being provided by the marriage couple themselves. The ways it was spent had also changed and might be used to set up an independent home.

If you get married to your cousin then the dowry is paid by the groom and also the bride's family. It depends where you are going to live and what is given. If they are going to live with the family then both sides will make a contribution. If they live on their own they will also make a contribution if they are working.

Looking to the future: children and dowries

Many of the women said they would not continue the practice of dowry with their own daughters and would not expect to receive one for their sons. Times were changing, they said, and as more and more women were earning, they would prefer to pay for their own marriages, along with their prospective husbands. In the past, the payment for the marriage fell completely on the bride's parents, but now the groom's parents contributed too. As a result, both sets of parents were likely to pay towards the marriage. A Sikh woman told me:

I think that because more women are working now they will contribute to their marriages just as the groom and his family will. It didn't used to be like that but now it is. I wouldn't want to do the dowry practice with my own children. I wouldn't want to give a dowry for my daughter and I wouldn't want anyone to give one for my son. I would like to think that both the bride and groom and their parents would pay for the marriage together, rather than it being the responsibility of just the bride's parents.

Although they spoke about dowry as a thing of the past, women wanted to maintain their identity as Asian women living in British society. A Hindu woman said,

Just because we don't see the value of dowries or believe in the giving of them it doesn't mean we want to forget about our identity. We are proud of who we are and where we come from. But our identity is changing because we have grown up here and some of our parents may have been born here as well. We want to keep our Asian identity, but we also want to change as well and because we live here it influences how we think and what we want to do with our lives.

However, some of the Muslim women maintained that the *mahr* would persist, as it was related to their religious practice. They also believed that the practice of dowries associated with inter-family marriage would continue:

If you are religious, then you will keep the *mahr*. But I also believe that the dowry will continue for some Muslims. It is a positive thing for many Muslim people because both families pay for it because they have an interest in their children.

Many of the women who had sons did not relish a continuation of dowries. They stressed that their own sons, being 'modern men', would challenge the stereotypes associated with Asian gender relations. A Sikh woman said,

I would like my son to be modern, that means that he would think that women were the same as them. As equal to them and they are not better than women, which is how a lot of Asian men are brought up. If they think like this then they will expect the dowry, but if they are more equal then they will think that both the bride and the groom's parents will and should pay for the wedding together.

This was also emphasised by a Hindu woman:

In years to come, do you think we will be doing the dowry thing? I don't think so, I don't want my children to continue the dowry with their own children and I won't be giving my children dowries either. I will contribute and get them expensive presents, but it will be the same as other cultures. The children can also contribute to the wedding.

The women saw their participation in higher education and consequently the labour market as giving them greater influence over their lives. They wanted more choice about whom they marry and in the practice of dowries, and they connected such freedom of choice to higher education as an agent for change. When they looked to the future lives of their children it was clear that attitudes and cultural expectations were shifting.

Dowries and shifting identities
Many of the women indicated that their identities were shifting in all respects. As second and third generation British, their identities were not like those of their mothers, as their lives were quite different. The notion of 'becoming like

English people' often came up in the interviews. Many of the women indicated that they felt that white British society wanted Asian people to abandon their cultural practices and become more like other British people. They felt that practices such as dowry giving were seen to be important by Asian communities but that non-Asians viewed them as 'alien' and 'different'.

One consequence of Asian families' migration to Western countries was the way Western culture assumed the power to *interpret* Eastern practices, which they then labelled as oppressive. Such misrepresentations of Asian cultures were linked to the othering of Asian communities. Because Asian communities did not conform to the values of white British society, their practices were seen to threaten notions of belonging to British society and interpreted as 'strange', thus helping decide who does not belong to British society. These notions of strangeness are reinforced by boundaries of acceptance and conformity, defined by the invisible presence of colonial ideals of bourgeois family life. In this sense, Asian women can be seen as being both inside and outside the boundaries of acceptance. They may be happy to conform to British values, yet they still want to maintain their own definitions of what it means to be *British Asian*.

A cultural shift in the giving of dowries means that presents given to the groom are now seen as the same as those given by western parents to their children on their wedding day. This shift in dowry practice is related to the shift in arranged marriages. Now that women have a greater say in who they will marry and often use their educational status to choose their husband, they are reshaping their participation in arranged marriages and dowries. They are negotiating a balance between maintaining traditional familial ties and community values and adopting certain individualistic British values. Although women want to hold on their familial ties and maintain their links to the community, the ways they do this is changing. They are constantly defining and re-defining what it means to be an Asian woman in British society. Whilst in the past their membership of particular social networks may have been well understood as largely constrained to immediate family and possibly religious interest groups, today their membership of different networks is more fluid and reaches well beyond the traditional family orientated groupings.

Asian communities in Britain are dealing with changes in economic and social circumstances by engaging in communities of practice and communities of belonging which help them shape these forms of belonging. The women's histories bind them together as members of their communities of practice, which have shared commonalities and in which they feel safe, secure and protected. Their commonalities ensure boundaries of identity which keep insiders in and outsiders out. Because it is within this context that changes for Asian women and their identity is taking place, the re-working of cultural practices is negotiated away from outsiders.

Some of the second and third generation women see themselves as belonging to wider society more than their parents ever did or do. Unlike their parents, they do not question their identity but they do see it as diverse. Their identity is based on their past experiences and future practices. They have complex affiliations with both British and Asian cultures. They see themselves as British, as Asian, as British Asian, Indian, Pakistani or Bangladeshi. They are not bound by an either/or option of identity but see their identity as ever changing and as combining both British and Asian modes of belonging. This identity gives them power.

Dowry practice is such a visible manifestation of an especially traditional aspect of Asian culture that it highlights the ambiguous minefield Asian women have to tread as they reconcile their identities. At its most traditional, dowry practice represents the most abject commodification of a woman; she is traded, at a price, in marriage. Having no economic value herself, she is sold to another family as a housekeeper and prospective mother. None of the respondents who discussed dowries would acknowledge that dowries could be interpreted in such a negative light today. Although they acknowledged the negative connotations of dowry practice, they minimised their impact, stressing the differences between the lives of their parents and their own lives today, and also the positive aspects of traditional values. Criticisms of dowries were considered acceptable if they came from within Asian culture but never when they came from people outside.

The changing face of dowry practice was directly related to the new status Asian women were finding for themselves and the new identities they were shaping to reflect that status, which affirmed these new identities as Asian women in Britain. The communities of practice developed within the university setting were important spaces for Asian women to share understandings of dowries and their common concerns about white British society, and to explore how these could be reconciled.

10

Conclusions

Much of this book has discussed the changes taking place in Asian communities in Britain in the twenty first century. These are observable phenomena that illustrate the growing confidence of Asian communities in Britain. Expectations have totally changed: whereas many first generation migrants anticipated returning to the sub-continent in later life, for their children and grandchildren such a move would be unthinkable. For them, Britain will always be their place of origin, even though they may retain strong cultural and religious affiliations to Asia. It may seem glib to simply contrast the 'traditional' perspective of the older generations with the 'modern' outlook of the young, but this is in many ways a fair interpretation of how Asian culture in Britain presents itself.

Many of the women in my study were aware that they, as young people, had adopted a modern approach to life and, moreover, that their parents pushed them towards a modern way of living. There are undoubtedly cultural differences between life 'back home' and life in Britain and this book starts at a point in time when what is deemed possible and desirable in young Asian people's lives is changing dramatically.

The physical link to the sub-continent has become more tenuous. Holidays back home to attend social functions and cement family ties are still common, but few migrants in the Asian community, even of the first generation, intend to return permanently. In global terms Asian families, like many others, find themselves stretched across two, three or even four continents and yet still closely linked, thanks to modern communication technology and international air transport. The 'traditional' world has in some ways simply ceased to exist.

The traditional elements that remain but are being renegotiated are the cultural practices around class and caste, how the family is organised, and the role of gender. It is here that Asian culture is most distinct from white British culture and it is gender roles that most differentiate the traditional outlook from the modern. The traditional role for Asian women used to be as homemakers and mothers; men assumed the superior role of breadwinner and patriarch. The impact of this traditional approach is often most stark in terms of the different status accorded to men and women in the marriage process and the customs surrounding dowries. In the modern western world the traditionally inferior position of Asian women has been undermined by economic and social pressures. Today there is greater expectation that British Asian women will engage in higher education and paid work and will have a significant role in choosing their marriage partners. Establishing an identity as an Asian woman that reconciles the traditional demands of their family patterns with the potential opportunities of successful modern life is an immense challenge to Asian communities in Britain today and will greatly affect Asian families' lives in the future.

When Asian women enter higher education, they are essentially doing something that is new to both Asian and British cultures. Not only does it flag up the modern role of Asian women within their own communities, but they are a new kind of student in the British Academy. However, they enter the Academy bearing an additional burden in the form of stereotypical understanding about 'traditional' Asian women held in white western culture. The assumptions in the Academy have not moved on: they are based on stereotyped views of an Asian culture characterised by the power of males over females, the subservient role of women in the family and their lack of choice of marriage partner. The outdated image of Asian women has been further entrenched by Government policy that fosters the perception of Asian women as victims of a backward culture that enforces unwelcome marriages with brutal honour killings. These views affirm the 'otherness' of Asian lives.

Within the Academy, Asian girls are understood as alien. The difference that is constructed is built around the wrong set of differences. The understanding of Asian women that still prevails in the Academy is based on misinformed ideas, partly on outdated notions that might have applied to their mothers or grandmothers, and partly on the worst excesses of the redtop press. Unsurprisingly, then, the Academy remains an alien environment for Asian women. For a start, the university environment is new to them – they are the first cohort to enter higher education in large numbers. Secondly, the Academy's perception of them is characterised by an alarmingly inaccurate understanding of who they really are. So no wonder Asian women have adopted strategies that will engender a sense of security and safety in this alien environment.

The white, middle class, male environment of the Academy contributes to Asian women's feelings of marginalisation at university. It has made them turn to support and friendship networks amongst other similar students. In their informal and frequent meetings, they build trusting and mutually supportive communities of practice to compensate for being unable to turn for support to either the Academy itself or to their traditional communities. Their parents and even their elder siblings have no experience of university. The unique circumstances of migration patterns and family histories means that large numbers of Asian women find themselves in universities where they must negotiate their place. They are compelled to rethink who they are and who they may become in the future. This they can do through their new communities of practice and social networks at the university.

The communities of practice the women build at university provide a third space of belonging and identity development. The spaces Asian women occupy in their home lives or the university lecture hall are loaded with ambiguous meanings about the relationship between traditional and modern life and between Asian and British culture. Engaging in a closed world in which problems are readily understood because of shared experiences makes it possible for them to devise strategies for coping with home life, university life and their expectations for the future.

The sense of belonging engendered by the community of practice and the third space help the women respond to the choices they have to make when going to university. They select universities that are generally local and have a good many students from similar ethnic, social and cultural backgrounds with whom they can readily identify. Their traditional communities see these institutions as a safer option than travelling away from home.

Although the women often put their decision to attend university down to their desire to 'improve themselves' or 'do well in life', and to achieve professional social mobility, university also gave them greater say in their personal lives and their choice of husband. Involvement in the wider social and friendship networks they formed at university developed their awareness of the wider impact of their choices. It was in this third space and within their communities of practice that they were able to reassess their social capital and rethink their identities.

Simply by attending university, their status within their family and traditional community changed dramatically and expectations about their earning potential rose. At university, Asian women use their agency to form powerful networks, and from the communities of practice they actively construct, they draw power to have agency within the university and, even more significantly, in their family lives and their prospects for the future.

Appendix – Respondent Details

M = mother, F = father

Name/Number	Age	Religion	Status	Parents' occupation
1 – Anya	20	Hindu	Single	M- housewife, F – postman
2 – Aisha	21	Hindu	Single	M-shop asst, F-cab business
3 – Saraya	20	Hindu	Single	M – lecturer, F-teacher
4 – Shilpa	22	Hindu	Single	M-teacher, F-social worker
5 – Sonia	23	Hindu	Single	M-teacher, F-teacher
6 – Leila	22	Hindu	Single	M-housewife, F-factory worker
7 – Jyoti	25	Hindu	Married	M-housewife, F-cab driver
8 – Nickita	20	Hindu	Single	M-housewife, F-factory worker
9 – Rani	21	Hindu	Single	M-bank asst, F-store manager
10 – Sabita	23	Hindu	Married	M-housewife, F-accounts clerk
11 – Sangeeta	21	Hindu	Single	M and F -shop owners
12 – Kali	22	Hindu	Single	M and F – factory owners
13 – Devi	21	Hindu	Single	M- machinist, F-manager
14 – Daksha	25	Hindu	Married	M- housewife, F-teacher
15 – Damini	22	Hindu	Single	M and F – social workers
16 – Tana	22	Hindu	Single	M and F – teachers
17 – Sureeta	23	Sikh	Single	M-teacher, F-solicitor
18 – Sunita	22	Sikh	Single	M-youth worker, F-teacher
19 – Jaswinder	21	Sikh	Single	M-nurse, F-FE lecturer
20 – Narinder	25	Sikh	Married	M-housewife, F-civil servant
21 – Kirtan	20	Sikh	Single	M-housewife, F-accountant
22 – Kuldip	21	Sikh	Single	M-mental health, F-social work
23 – Pinky	22	Sikh	Single	M-housewife, F-salesman
24 – Jaswant	23	Sikh	Single	M-nurse, F-teacher
25 – Julee	25	Sikh	Married	M-housewife, F-own business
26 – Jatinder	20	Sikh	Single	M and F – teachers
27 – Preeta	21	Sikh	Single	M and F – accountants
28 – Balgit	23	Sikh	Single	M-housewife, F- law student
29 – Amee	20	Sikh	Single	M-housewife, F-factory worker
30 – Surinder	20	Sikh	Single	M-housewife, F-teacher

Name/Number	Age	Religion	Status	Parents' occupation
31 – Dalgit	22	Sikh	Single	M-housewife, F-banker
32 – Permjit	23	Sikh	Single	M and F – teachers
33 – Yasmin	24	Muslim	Married	M and F- own business
34 – Farah	24	Muslim	Married	M-housewife, F-businessman
35 – Farzana	25	Muslim	Married	M-nursery nurse, F-teacher
36 – Ayan	21	Muslim	Single	M-housewife, F-builder
37 – Shinaz	22	Muslim	Single	M-housewife, F-teacher
38 – Salima	23	Muslim	Single	M-housewife, F-cab driver
39 – Sofia	22	Muslim	Single	M-housewife, F-factory work
40 – Alia	21	Muslim	Single	M-housewife, F-retail manager
41 – Ameena	23	Muslim	Single	M-teacher, F-accountant
42 – Bibi	20	Muslim	Single	M-teacher, F-lecturer
43 – Dalia	22	Muslim	Single	M-housewife, F-builder
44 – Hannah	22	Muslim	Single	M-housewife, F-factory work
45 – Jamila	23	Muslim	Single	M-housewife, F-builder

References

Abbas, T. (2004) *The Education of British South Asians*. London: Palgrave.

Afshar, H. (1994) 'Muslim Women in West Yorkshire', in H. Afshar and M. Maynard (eds.) *The Dynamics of Race and Gender*. London: Taylor and Francis.

Ahier, J., Chaplain, R., Linfield, R., Moore, R., and Williams, J. (2000) 'School Work Experience: Young People and the Labour Market', *Journal of Education and Work* 13 (3): 273-288.

Ahmad, F. (2003) 'Still in Progress? Methodological Dilemmas, Tensions and Contradictions in Theorising South Asian Muslim Women', in N. Puwar and P. Raghuram (eds.) *South Asian Women in the Diaspora*. Oxford: Berg.

Ahmad, F., Modood, T. and Lissenburgh, S. (2003) *South Asian Women and Employment in Britain: The Interaction of Gender and Ethnicity*. London: PSI.

Alexander, C. (2000) *The Asian Gang: Ethnicity, Identity, Masculinity*. Oxford: Berg.

Allen, K. and Walker, A. (1992) 'A Feminist Analysis of Interviews with Elderly Mothers and their Daughters', in J. Gilgun, K. Daly and G. Handel (eds.) *Qualitative Methods in Family Research*. Newbury Park, CA: Sage.

Amit, V. (ed.) (2002) *Realising Community: Concepts, Social Relationships and Sentiments*. London: Routledge.

Anderson, K. and Umberson, D. (2004) 'Gendering Violence: Masculinity and Power in Men's accounts of Domestic Violence', in S. Hesse-Biber and M. Yaiser (eds.) *Feminist Perspectives on Social Research*. Oxford: Oxford University Press.

Andersen, B. (1983) *Imagined Communities: Reflections on the Origins and Spread of Nationalism*. London: Verso.

Anthias, F. and Yuval-Davis, N. (1992) *Racialised Boundaries: Race, Nation, Gender, Colour and Class and the Anti-Racist Struggle*. London: Routledge.

Anwar, M. (1979) *The Myth of Return*. London: Heinemann.

Anwar, M. (1998) *Between Two Cultures*. London: Routledge.

Archer, L. (2002) 'Change, Culture and Tradition: British Muslim Pupils talk about Muslim girls post-16 choices', *Race, Ethnicity and Education* 5 (4): 359-376.

Archer, L. and Leathwood, C. (2003) 'Identities, Inequalities and Higher Education', in L. Archer, M. Hutchings and A. Ross (eds.) *Higher Education and Social Class: Issues of Exclusion and Inclusion*. London: Routledge Falmer.

Back, L. (1996) *New Ethnicities and Urban Culture: Racisms and Multiculture in Young Lives*. London: UCL Press.

Bagguley, P. and Hussain, Y. (2007) *The Role of Higher Education in Providing Opportunities for South Asian Women*. Bristol: JRF.

Balatti, J. and Falk, I. (2002) 'Socioeconomic contributions of adult learning to community: a social capital perspective', *Adult Education* 4 (52): 281 – 298.

Ballard, R. (1978) 'The Political Economy of Migration', in J. Eade (ed.) *Migrants, Workers and the Social Order.* London: Tavistock.

Ballard, R. (1994) *Desh Pardesh: The South Asian Presence in Britain.* Oxford: Hurst.

Barke, M., Braidford, P., Houston, M., Hunt, A., Lincoln, I., Morphet, C., Stone, I. and Walker, A. (2000) *Students in the Labour Market: Nature, Extent and Implications of term-time Employment among University of Northumbria Graduates.* London: DfEE.

Barrett, M. (1980) *Women's Oppression Today: Problems in Marxist Feminist Analysis.* London: Verso.

Barth, F. (1969) 'Introduction', in F. Barth (ed.) *Ethnic Groups and Boundaries: The Social Organisation of Culture Difference.* London: George Allen and Unwin.

Basit, T. (1997) *Eastern Values, Western Milieu: Identities and Aspirations of Adolescent British Muslim Girls.* Aldershot: Ashgate.

Bauman, Z. (2001) *Community: Seeking Safety in an Insecure World.* Cambridge: Polity.

Baumann, G. (1996) *Contested Cultures: Discourses of Identity in Multi-Ethnic London.* Cambridge: Cambridge University Press.

BBC *Today Programme* Radio 4, March 2008.

Beck, U. (1992) *Risk Society: Towards a New Modernity.* London: Sage.

Bell, S. and Coleman, S. (1999) *The Anthropology of Friendship.* Oxford: Berg.

Berthoud, R. (2000) 'Ethnic Employment Penalties in Britain', *Journal of Ethnic and Migration Studies*, 26 (3): 389-416.

Bhachu, P. (1985) *Twice Migrants: East African Sikh Settlers in Britain.* London: Tavistock.

Bhachu, P. (1988) 'Apni Marzi Gardi: Sikh Women in Britain' in S. Westwood and P. Bhachu (eds.) *Enterprising Women: Ethnicity, Economy and Gender Relations.* London: Routledge.

Bhachu, P. (1991) 'Culture, Ethnicity and Class among Punjabi Sikh women in the 1990s', *New Community* 17 (3): 401-12.

Bhat, P. and Halli, S. (1999) 'Demography of Brideprice and Dowry: Causes and Consequences of the Indian Marriage Squeeze', *Population Studies* 53: 129-144.

Bhatia, N. (2003) Romantic Transgressions in the Colonial Zone, in: N. Puwar and P. Raghuram (eds.) *South Asian Women in the Diaspora* (Oxford, Berg) 99-116.

Bhatti, G. (1999) *Asian Children at Home and School.* London: Routledge.

Bhopal, K. (1997) *Gender, 'Race' and Patriarchy: A Study of South Asian Women.* Aldershot: Ashgate.

Bhopal, K. (2003) 'Patriarchy in the 21st Century: A Relevant or Redundant Concept?', *Pakistan Journal of Women's Studies* 10 (1): 5-21.

Bhopal, K. (2008) 'Shared communities and shared understandings: the experiences of Asian women in a British university'. *International Studies in Sociology of Education, Special Issue The Struggle for Equality: the intersection of class, race, gender and disability.* 18, (3 & 4), 185-197.

Bhopal, K. (2009) 'Identity, empathy and 'otherness': Asian women, education and dowries in the UK' in *Race, Ethnicity and Education, Special Issue Black Feminisms and Postcolonial Paradigms: Researching Educational Inequalities.* 12, 1: 27-40.

Bhopal, K. and Myers, M. (2008) *Insiders, Outsiders and Others: Gypsies and Identity.* Hertfordshire: University of Hertfordshire Press.

Boserup, E. (1970) *Women in Economic Development.* New York: St. Martins Press.

Bradley, H. (1996) *Fractured Identities: Changing Patterns of Inequality.* Oxford: Basil Blackwell.

Brah, A. (1993) "Race' and 'Culture' in the Gendering of Labour Markets: South Asian young Muslim Women in the Labour Market", *New Community* 29: 441-458.

Brah, A. (1996) *Cartographies of Diaspora: Contesting Identities.* London: Routledge.

Brah, A. and Minhas, R. (1985) 'Structural Racism or Cultural Conflict: Asian Girls in British Schools', G. Weiner (ed.) *Just a Bunch of Girls.* Milton Keynes: Open University Press.

Britton, C. and Baxter, A. (1999) 'Becoming a Mature Student: gendered narratives of the self', *Gender and Education* 11 (2): 179-193.

Broadbridge, A., Swanson, V. and Taylor, C. (2000) 'Retail Change: Effects on Employees' Job Demands and Home Life', *International Review of Retail, Distribution and Consumer Research* 10 (4): 417-432.

Broude, G. (1994) *Marriage, Family and Relationships.* Santa Barbara: Abc-Clio.

Brown, G. Bhrolchain, M. and Harris, T. (1975) 'Social Class and Psychiatric Disturbance among Women in an Urban Population', *Sociology* 9: 225-254.

Buie, E. (2000) 'Students find Ill-health on the Curriculum', *Glasgow Herald* 29 March: 3.

Burda, P., Vaux, A. and Schill, T. (1984) 'Social Support Resources: Variation across Sex and Sex Role' *Personality and Social Psychology Bulletin* 10: 119-126.

Bynner, J, Ferri, E. and Shepard, P. (1997) *Twenty-Something in the 1990s: Getting on, Getting by, Getting nowhere.* Aldershot: Ashgate.

Byrne, A. and Lentin. R. (2000) *(Re)Searching Women: Feminist Research Methodologies in the Social Sciences.* Dublin: IPA.

Callender, C. and Jackson, J. (2005) 'Does the Fear of Debt Deter Students from Higher Education?', *Journal of Social Policy* 34 (4): 509-540.

Callender, C. and Kemp, M. (2000) *Changing Student Finances: Income, Expenditure and the take-up of Student Loans among Full and Part-time Higher Education Students in 1998/1999.* London: DfEE.

Callender, C. and Wilkinson, D. (2003) *2003/03 Student Income and Expenditure Survey: Students' Income, Expenditure and Debt in 2002/03 and Changes since 1998/99.* London: DfES.

Campbell, R. and Wasco, S. (2000) 'Feminist Approaches to Social Sciences: Epistemological and Methodological Tenents', *American Journal of Community Psychology* 28 (6): 773-791.

Campbell, C. and McLean, C. (2002) 'Ethnic identities, social capital and health inequalities: factors shaping African-Caribbean participation in local community networks in the UK', *Social Science and Medicine* 55 (4): 643-657.

Carby, H. (1982) 'White Woman Listen! Black Feminism and the Boundaries of Sisterhood', in *CCCS The Empire Strikes Back.*

Carmichael, F. and Woods, R. (2000) 'Ethnic Penalties in Unemployment and Occupational Attainment: Evidence for Britain', *International Review of Applied Economics*, 14 (1): 71-97.

Charsley, K. (2003) Rishtas: Transnational Marriages in Pakistan. Unpublished PhD Thesis: University of Edinburgh.

Charsley, K. (2005) 'Vulnerable Brides and Transnational Ghar Damads: Gender, Risk and Adjustment among Pakistani Migrants to Britain', *Indian Journal of Gender Studies* 12 (2): 381-406.

Charmaz, K. (2006) *Constructing Grounded Theory.* London: Sage.

Chavis, D. and Wandersman, A. (1990) 'Sense of Community in the Urban Environment: A Catalyst for Participation and Community Development', *American Journal of Community Psychology* 18 (1): 55-81.

Cheng, Y. and Heath, A. (1993) 'Ethnic Origins and Class Destinations', *Oxford Review of Education* 19 (2): 151-165.

Christie, H. and Munro, M. (2003) 'The Logic of Loans: Students' Perceptions of the Costs and Benefits of the Student Loan', *British Journal of Sociology of Education* 24 (5): 621-636.

Clark, K. and Drinkwater, D. (2007) 'Some Preliminary Findings on Ethnic Minority Labour Market Activity using Controlled Access Microdata', *SARS Newsletter,* February.

Cohen, S. and Wells, T. (1985) 'Stress, Social Support and the Buffering Hypothesis', *Psychological Bulletin* 98: 310-357.

Coffield, F. and Vignoles, A. (1997) *Widening Participation in Higher Education by Gender, Ethnicity and Age.* Report of the National Committee of Inquiry into Higher Education.

Coleman, J. (1988) 'Social Capital and the Creation of Human Capital', *American Journal of Sociology* 94: S1-S95.

Coleman, C. (2005) 'Amazing Double Life a Growing Trend among Muslim Girls', *The Daily Mail,* 25 March.

Collins, P. (1990) *Black Feminist Thought: Knowledge, Consciousness and the Politics of Empowerment.* London: Harper Collins.

Connor, H., Tyers, C., Modood, T., and Hillage, J. (2004) *Why the Difference? A Closer Look at Higher Education Minority Ethnic Students and Graduates.* London: DfES.

Cox, E. (1998) *A Truly Civil Society.* Australia: Boyer Lectures.

Cutrona, C. (1986) 'Objective Determinants of Perceived Social Support', *Journal of Personality and Social Psychology* 50: 349-355.

Dale, A., Shaheen, N., Fieldhouse, E. and Kalra, V. (2002) 'Routes into Education and Employment for Young Bangladeshi and Pakistani Women in the UK', *Ethnic and Racial Studies* 25, 6: 942-968.

Das Gupta, M. (1987) 'Selective Discrimination against Female Children in Rural Punjab India', *Research Paper,* Dhaka India.

Davidson, W. and Cotter, P. (1991) 'The Relationship between Sense of Community and Subjective Well-Being: A First Look', *American Journal of Community Psychology* 19: 246-253.

Davies, P. (1995) 'Response or Resistance? Access Students and Government Policies on Admissions', *Journal of Access Studies* 10 (1): 72-80.

Davies, R. and Elias, P. (2003) *Dropping Out: A Study of Early Leavers from Higher Education.* London: DfES.

Devault, M. (1990) 'Talking and Listening from a Woman's Standpoint: Feminist Strategies for Interviewing and Analysis', *Social Problems* 37 (1): 96-116.

Donnan, H. (1988) *Marriage Among Muslims.* Delhi: Hindustan Publications.

Drury, B. (1991) 'Sikh Girls and the Maintenance of an Ethnic Culture', *New Community,* 17 (3): 387-399.

Dunbar, C. Rodriquez, D. and Parker, L. (2002) 'Race, Subjectivity and the Interview Process', in J. Gubrium and J. Holstein (eds.) *Handbook of Interview Research.* Thousand Oaks, CA: Sage.

Edlund, L. (2006) 'The Marriage Squeeze: Interpretations of Dowry and Inflation', *Journal of Political Economy* 15: 1327-1333.

Edwards, R. (1993) *Mature Women Students: Separating or Connecting Family and Education.* London: Taylor and Francis.

Ensel, W. and Lin, N. (1991) 'The Life Stress Paradigm and Psychological Distress', *Journal of Health and Social Behaviour* 32: 321-341.

Etzioni, A. (1993) *The Spirit of Community: Rights, Responsibilities and the Communitarian Agenda.* New York: Crown.

Everard, K., Lach, H., Fisher, E. and Baum, C. (2000) 'Relationship of Activity and Social Support to the Functional Health of Older Adults', *Journal of Gerontology* 55: S208-S212.

Federation of Student Islamic Societies (2005) *The Muslim Student Survey*. London: FOSIS.

Finch, J. (1984) 'It's Great to Have Someone to Talk to: Women Interviewing Women', in C. Bell and H. Roberts (eds.) *Social Researching: Politics, Problems, Practice*. London: RKP.

Fischer, M. and Lyon, W. (2000) 'Marriage Strategies in Lahore', in M. Bock and A. Rao (eds.) *Culture, Creation and Procreation: Concepts of Kinship in South Asian Practice*. Oxford: Berghahn Books.

Fonow, M. and Cook, J. (1991) 'Back to the Future: A Look at the Second Wave of Feminist Epistemology and Methodology', in M. Fonow and J. Cook (eds.) *Beyond Methodology: Feminist Scholarship as Lived Research*. Bloomington: Indiana University Press.

Fontana, A. and Frey, J. (2005) 'The Interview: From Neutral Stance to Political Involvement' in N. Denzin and Y. Lincoln (eds.) *The Sage Handbook of Qualitative Research*. Thousand Oaks, CA: Sage.

Forsyth, A. and Furlong, A. (2003) *Losing Out? Socioeconomic Disadvantage and Experience in Further and Higher Education*. Bristol: Policy.

Francescato, D. and Ghirelli, G. (1998) *Community Psychology*. Rome: Nova Italia Scientifica.

Gardner, K. and Shukur, A. (1994) 'I'm British, I'm Bengali and I'm living here', in R. Ballard and M. Banks (eds.) *Desh Pardesh: The South Asian Presence in Britain*. Oxford: Hurst.

Giddens, A. (1985) *The Nation State and Violence*. Cambridge: Polity.

Grant, B. (1997) 'Disciplining Students: the Construction of Student Subjectivities', *British Journal of Sociology of Education* 18 (1): 101-114.

Ghuman P. (1994) *Coping With Two Cultures*. Bristol: Longdum.

Goodwin, R. (1999) *Personal Relationships across Cultures*. London: Routledge.

Goody, J. (1973). 'Bridewealth and Dowry in Africa and Eurasia.' *Cambridge Papers in Social Anthropology.*

Green, A., Owen, D. and Wilson, R. (2005) *Changing Patterns of Employment by Ethnic Group and for Migrant Workers*. London: Learning Council.

Gusfield, J. (1975) *The Community: A Critical Response.* New York: Harper Colophon.

Hall, S. (1990) 'Cultural Identity and Diaspora', in J. Rutherford (ed.) *Identity: Community, Culture, Difference.* London: Sage.

Hall, S. (1996) 'Introduction: who needs identity?', in S. Hall and P. du Gay (eds.) *Questions of Cultural Identity*. London: Sage.

Hatcher, R. (1998) 'Class Differentiation in Education: Rational Choices?' *British Journal of Sociology of Education* 19 (1): 5-24.

Hazareesingh, S. (1986) 'Racism and Cultural Identity: an Indian Perspective', *Dragons Teeth*, 24.

Hesse-Biber, S. and Leavy, L. (2005) *The Practice of Qualitative Research*. Thousand Oaks, CA: Sage.

Hobfoll, S. and Stokes, S. (1988) 'The Process and Mechanics of Social Support', in S. Duck (ed.) *Handbook of Personal Relationships*. Oxford: Wiley.

Home Office (2001) *Community Cohesion: A Report of Independent Review led by Ted Cantle.* London: HMSO.

Home Office (2002) *A Choice by Right: The Report of the Working Group on Forced Marriage.* London: HMSO.

Home Office (2002) *Secure Borders, Safe Havens: Integration with Diversity in Modern Britain.* London: HMSO.

Home Office (2003) *Education for Citizenship and the teaching of Democracy in Schools: Final Report of the Advisory Group on Citizenship, led by Sir Bernard Crick.* London: HMSO.

hooks, b. (1982) *Ain't I A Woman?* London: Pluto.

Hudson, M. and Sahin-Dikmen, M. (2007) *Network on Ethnicity and Women Scientists*. London: PSI.

Hurlbert, J. and Acock, A. (1990) 'The Effects of Marital Status on the Form and Composition of Social Networks', *Social Science Quarterly* 71: 163-174.

Hutchings, M. and Archer, A. (2001) 'Higher than Einstein: Constructions of going to University among Working Class Non-participants', *Research Papers in Education* 16 (1): 69-91.

Islam for Today (2008) Payments to and from the Bride in Islamic Law and Tradition.

Jeffrey, P. and Jeffrey, R. (1996) *Don't Marry me to a Plowman!* Oxford: Westview.

Jenkins, R. (2002) *Foundations of Sociology: Towards a Better Understanding of the Human World.* Basingstoke: Palgrave Macmillan.

Jewkes, R., Penn-Kekana, K. and Rose-Junius, H. (2005) 'If They Rape Me, I Can't Blame Them: Reflections on Gender in the Context of Child Rape', *Social Science and Medicine* 61: 1809-1820.

Jhutti, J. (1998) 'Dowry among Sikhs in Britain', in V. Menski (ed.) *South Asians and the dowry problem,* New Delhi: Vistaar Publications, 175-98.

Kapadia, K. (1995) *Siva and her Sisters.* Boulder: Westview.

Kawale, R. (2003) 'A kiss is just a kiss...or is it? South Asian lesbian and bisexual women and the construction of space', in N. Puwar and P. Raghuram (eds.) *South Asian Women in the Diaspora.* Oxford, Berg.

Keller, S. (2003) *Community: Pursuing the Dream.* Princeton, NJ: Princeton University Press.

Kessler, R. and Essex, M. (1982) 'Marital Status and Depression: The Importance of Coping Resources', *Social Forces* 61: 484-507.

Khan, V. (1979) *Minority Families in Britain.* London: Macmillan.

Kilpatrick, S., Bell, R. and Falk, I. (1999) 'The Role of Group Learning in Building Social Capital', *Journal of Vocational Education and Training* 51 (1): 129-144.

Klandermans, B. (1997) 'How Group Identification helps to Overcome the Dilemma of Collective Action', *American Behavioural Scientist* 45 (5) 887-900.

Krishanaswamy, S. (1995) 'Dynamics of personal and social factors influencing the attitude of married and unmarried working women towards dowry', *International Journal of Sociology of the Family* 25 (1): 31-42.

Kumar, V. (2003) 'Poisoning Deaths in Married Women', *Journal of Clinical Forensic Medicine* 11 (2): 2-5.

Kumari, R. (1989) *Brides are not for Burning: Dowry Victims in India.* London: Sangahm.

Kawale, R. (2003) 'A Kiss is just a kiss or is it? South Asian Lesbian and Bisexual Women and the Construction of Space', in N. Puwar and P. Ragthuram (eds) *South Asian Women in the Diaspora.* London, Berg.

Lave, J. and Wenger, E. (1991) *Situated learning: Legitimate peripheral participation.* Cambridge: Cambridge University Press.

Leslie, L. and Grady, K. (1985) 'Changes in Mothers' Social Support Following Divorces', *Journal of Marriage and Family* August: 663-673.

Lewis, G. and Neal, S. (2005) *Migration and Citizenship, Ethnic and Racial Studies, Special Issue,* 28 (3).

Liem, R. and Liem, J. (1978) 'Social Class and Mental Illness Reconsidered: the Role of Economic Stress and Social Support' *Journal of Health and Social Behaviour* 19: 139-156.

Lynch, K. and O'Riordan, C. (1998) 'Inequality in Higher Education: A Study of Class Barriers', *British Journal of Sociology of Education* 19 (4): 445-478.

MacMillan, D. and Chavis, D. (1986) 'Sense of Community: A Definition and Theory', *Journal of Community Psychology* 14 (6): 6-23.

Malhotra, A. and Mathar, M. (1997) 'Women's Domestic Power: the Importance of Life Course History and the Marriage System in India' Annual Meeting of the Population Association, USA.

Malik, S. (2005) 'Girls Just Wanna Have Fun', *Q-News,* Issue 36.

Mand, K. (2006) 'Gender, Ethnicity and Social Narratives in the support of Elderly Sikh Men and Women', *Ethnic and Racial Studies* 29 (6): 1057-1071.

Mandelbaum, P. (1999), 'Dowry deaths in India: let only your corpse come out of that house', *Commonwealth* 126 (17):18-19,

Marsden, P. (1997) 'Core Discussion Networks of Americans', *American Sociological Review* 52: 122-131.

Martini, E. and Sequi, R. (1995) *Local Community.* Rome: Nova Italia Scientifica.

Matthew, A. (1987) 'Attitudes towards Dowry', *Indian Journal of Social Work* 13 (4) 66-72.

McCiod, C. (1989) *Dowry Deaths in India.* Michigan: Michigan State University.

McKechnie, J., Hobbs, S. and Lindsay, S. (1998) 'The Nature and Extent of Student Employment at the University of Paisley', in P. Kelly (ed.) *Working in Two Worlds: Students and Part-time Employment.* Glasgow: Scottish Low Pay Unit.

Menon, R. and Bhasin, K. (1998) *Borders and Boundaries.* New Jersey: Rutgers.

Menski, W. (1988) *South Asians and the Dowry Problem.* Stoke on Trent: Trentham.

Meyer, D. (2001) 'The Poorest Years of your Life', *Times Higher Education Supplement* 30 March: 16.

Mirza, H. (1992) *Young, Female and Black.* London: Routledge.

Mirza, H. (1997) *Black British Feminism.* London: Routledge.

Modi, A. (2003) 'Where Love Dies First', *The Hindu Magazine* November.

Modood, T., Berthooud, R., Lakey, J., Nazroo, J., Smith, P., Virdee, S. and Beishon, S. (1997) *Diversity and Disadvantage: Fourth National Survey of Ethnic Minorities.* London: PSI.

Modood, T. (1988) '"Black" Racial Equality and Asian Identity', *New Community,* 14 (3).

Modood, T. (2006) 'Ethnicity Muslims and Higher Education Entry in Britain', *Teaching in Higher Education.*

Modood, T. and Shiner, M. (1994) *Ethnic Minorities and Higher Education: Why are there Differential Rates of Entry?* London: PSI.

Mooney, N. (2006) 'Aspiration, Reunification and Gender Transformation in Jat Sikh Marriages from India to Canada', *Global Networks* 6 (4): 389-402.

Moore, G. (1990) 'Structural Determinants of Men's and Women's Personal Networks', *American Sociological Review* 55: 726-735.

Moran-Ellis, J. (1996) 'Close to Home: The Experience of Researching Child Sexual Abuse', in M. Hester., L. Kelly and J. Radford (eds.) *Women, Violence and Male Power: Feminist Activism, Research and Practice.* Buckingham: Open University Press.

Moreau, M. and Leathwood, C. (2006) 'Balancing Paid Work and Studies: Working (-class) Students in Higher Education', *Studies in Higher Education* 31 (1): 23-42.

Oakley, A. (1981) 'Interviewing Women: A Contradiction in Terms', in H. Roberts (ed.) *Doing Feminist Research.* London: RKP.

Oakley, A. (2000) *Experiments in Knowing.* Bristol: Polity.

Oldenburg, V. (2002) *Dowry Murder.* Oxford: Oxford University Press.

ONS (Office of National Statistics) *Social Trends No. 24.* London: ONS.

ONS (Office of National Statistics) *Social Trends No. 36*. London: ONS.

Palriwala, R. and Risseeu, C. (1996) *Shifting Circles of Support*. New Delhi: Sage.

Parekh, B. (2008) *A New Politics of Identity. Political Principles for an Interdependent World*. London: Palgrave Macmillan.

Parmar, P. (1988) 'Gender, Race and Power: The Challenge to Youth Work Practice', in P. Cohen and H. Bains (eds.) *Multiracist Britain*. London: RKP.

Paul, M. (1985) *Dowry and the Position of Women in India*. New Delhi: Inter India Publications.

Phillipson, C.. Ahmed, N. and Latimer, J. (2003) *Women in Transition: A Study of the Experience of Bangladeshi Women living in Tower Hamlets*. Bristol: Policy Press.

Portes, A. (1998) 'Social Capital: Its Origins and Applications in Modern Sociology', *Annual Review of Sociology* 24: 1-24.

Prasad, B. (1994) 'Dowry-related Violence: a comparison of newspaper reports', *Journal of Comparative Family Studies* 25 (1): 75-88.

Pugliesi, K. (1989) 'Social Support and Self-esteem as Intervening Variables in the Relationship Between Social Roles and Women's Well-Being', *Community Mental Health Journal* 25: 87-100.

Pugliesi, K. and Shook, S. (1998) 'Gender, Ethnicity and Network Characteristics: Variation in Social Support Resources', *Sex Roles* 38 (3): 215-238.

Putnam, R. (1993) *Making Democracy Work: Civic Traditions in Modern Italy*. Princeton NJ: Princeton University Press.

Putnam, R. (2000) *Bowling Alone: The Collapse and Revival of American Community*. New York: Simon and Schuster.

Puwar, N. (2004) *Space Invaders: race, gender and bodies out of place*. Oxford: Berg.

Raghuram, P. (2003) Fashioning the South Asian Diaspora: production and consumption tales, in N. Puwar and P. Raghuram (eds.) *South Asian Women in the Diaspora*. Oxford, Berg.

Ramji, H. (2007) 'Dynamics of Religion and Gender amongst Young British Muslims', *Sociology*, 41 (6): 1171-1189.

Ray, K. (2000) 'Contested Terrain: Constructions of Race and Gender in Local Politics'. PhD Dissertation: University of Manchester.

Read, B., Archer, L. and Leathwood, C. (2003) 'Challenging Cultures: Student Conceptions of 'belonging' and Power at a Post-1992 University', *Studies in Higher Education* 28 (3).

Reay, D. (1998)'Always Knowing and Never Being Sure: Institutional and Family Habituses and Higher Education Choice', *Journal of Education Policy* 13 (4): 519-529.

Reay, D., David, M. and Ball, S. (2005) *Degrees of Choice: Social Class, Race and Gender in Higher Education*. Stoke on Trent: Trentham.

Reay, D., Davies, J., David, M. and Ball, S. (2001) 'Choices of Degree or Degrees of Choice? Social Class, Race, and the Higher Education Choice Process', *Sociology* 35 (4): 855-874.

Reddy, P. (1988) 'Consanguineous marriages and marriage payment: a study among three South Indian caste groups' *Annals of Human Biology* 15 (4): 263-245.

Redfield, R. (1971) *The Little Community*. New York: Harper.

Reinharz, S. and Chase, S. (2002) 'Interviewing Women', in J. Gubrium and J. Holstein (eds.) *Handbook of Interview Research*. Thousand Oaks, CA: Sage.

Renzetti, C. (1997) 'Confessions of a Reformed Positivist', in M. Schwartz (ed.) *Researching Sexual Violence Against Women*. Thousand Oaks, CA: Sage.

Reynolds, M. (2000) 'Bright Lights and the Pastoral Idyll: Ideas of Community underlying Management Educational Methodologies', *Management Learning* 31 (1): 670-681.

REFERENCES

Robertson, D. and Hillman, J. (1997) *Widening Participation in Higher Education for Students from Lower Socio-Economic Groups and Students with Disabilities.* Report 6 for the National Commission of Inquiry into Higher Education. London: HMSO.

Sales, R. (2005) 'Secure Borders, Safe Havens'? *Ethnic and Racial Studies* 28 (1): 445-462.

Samad, Y. and Eade, J. (2002) *Community Perceptions of Forced Marriage.* London: Foreign and Commonwealth Office.

Sarason, B., Shearin, E., Pierce, G., and Sarason, I. (1987) 'Interrelations of Social Support Measures: Theoretical and Practical Implications', *Journal of Personality and Social Psychology* 12: 813-822.

Sarason, S. (1974) *The Psychological Sense of Community: Prospects for a Community Psychology.* San Francisco, CA: Jossey-Bass.

Seth, S. (1995) 'Education of Asian Women', in M. Hughes and M. Kennedy (eds.) *New Futures: Changing Women's Education.* London: Routledge.

Shain, F. (2003) *The Schooling and Identity of Asian Girls.* Stoke on Trent: Trentham.

Sharma, U. (1984) *Dowry in north India: Its consequences for women as property.* St. Martin's Press: New York.

Shaw, A. (1988) *A Pakistani Community in Britain.* London: Basil Blackwell.

Shaw, A. (2000) *Kinship and Continuity: Pakistani Families in Britain.* Amsterdam: Harwood Academic.

Shiner, M. and Modood, T. (2002) 'Help or Hindrance? Higher Education and the Route to Ethnic Equality', *British Journal of Sociology of Education*, 32 (2): 209-232.

Siddiqui, H. (2003) 'It was written in her Kismet: Forced Marriage', in R. Gupta (ed.) *Homebreakers to Jailbreakers: Southall Black Sisters.* London: Zed Books.

Simpson, L., Purdam, K., Tajar, A., Fieldhouse, E., Gavalas, V., Tranmer, M., Pritchard, J. and Dorling, D. (2006) *Ethnic Minority Populations and the Labour Market: An Analysis of the 1991 and 2001 Census.* London: DWP.

Singh, G. and Tatla, D. (2006) *Sikhs in Britain: The Making of a Community.* London: Zed Books.

Srinivas, M. (1984) *Some Reflections on Dowry.* New Delhi: Oxford University Press.

Srinivasan, P. and Lee, G. (2004) The Dowry System in Northern India: Women's Attitudes to Change', *Journal of Marriage and Family* 66 (5): 1108-1117.

Stone, L. and James, C. (1995) 'Dowry, Bride-Burning and Female Power in India', *Women's Studies International Forum* 18 (2): 125-134.

Stopes-Roe, M. and Cochrane, R. (1990) *Citizens of This Country: The Asian British.* Clevedon: Multilingual Matters.

Strategy Unit (2003) *Ethnic Minorities and Labour Market.* London: Cabinet Office.

Strauss, A. and Corbin, J. (1990) *Basics of Qualitative Research.* London: Sage.

Teja, M. (1991). *Dowry: A Study of Attitudes and Practices.* New Delhi, India: Inter-India.

Tett, L. (2000) 'I'm Working Class and Proud of it: Gendered Experiences of Non-Traditional Participants in Higher Education', *Gender and Education* 12 (2): 183-194.

Tomlinson, S. (2005) 'Race, Ethnicity and Education under New Labour', *Oxford Review of Education* 31 (1): 153-171.

Tonnies, F. (1887) *Community and Civil Society.* Cambridge: Cambridge University Press.

Topolsky, J. (1999) 'On target, on task, on reflection: The culture of learning communities', Plenary of the International Conference Community Development Society, Athens: Georgia.

Turner, R. and Noh, S. (1983) 'Class and Psychological Vulnerability among Women: The Significance of Social Support and Personal Control' *Journal of Health and Social Behaviour* 24: 16-29.

Tyrer, D. and Ahmad, F. (2005) *Muslim Women and Higher Education: Identities, Experiences, Prospects.* Liverpool: European Social Fund.

Walby, S. (1990) *Theorising Patriarchy.* Oxford: Basil Blackwell.

Walton-Roberts, M. (2003) 'Transnational Geographies: Indian Immigration to Canada', *The Canadian Geographer* 47 (3): 235-250.

Walton-Roberts, M. (2004) 'Rescaling Citizenship: Gendering Canadian Immigration Policy', *Political Geography* 23: 265-281.

Warr, D. (2004) 'Stories in the Flesh and Voices in the Head: Reflections on the Context and Impact of Research with Disadvantaged Populations', *Qualitative Health Research* 14 (4): 578-587.

Watson, J. (1977) *Between Two Cultures.* Oxford: Basil Blackwell.

Weeks, J. (2000) *Making Sexual History.* Cambridge: Polity Press.

Werbner, P. (1990) *The Migration Process: Capital, Goods and Offerings Among British Pakistanis.* Oxford: Berg.

Werbner, P. (1996) 'Stamping the Earth with the Name of Allah: Zikr and the Sacralizing of Space among British Muslims', *Cultural Anthropology* 11 (3): 309-338.

Werbner, P. (2002) *Imagined Diasporas among Manchester Muslims.* Oxford: James Currey.

Werbner, P. (2005) 'Honour, Shame and the Politics of Sexual Embodiment among South Asian Muslims in Britain and Beyond: An Analysis of Debates in the Public Sphere', *International Social Science Review* 6 (1): 25-47.

Wenger, E. (1998) *Communities of Practice: Learning, Meaning, Identity.* Cambridge: Cambridge University Press.

Wenger, E. and Synder, W. (2000) 'Communities of Practice: The Organisational Frontier', *Harvard Business Review* 78 (1): 139-145.

Wilson, A. (1978) *Finding A Voice: Asian Women in Britain.* London: Virago.

Wilson, A. (2006) *Dreams, Questions, Struggles: Asian Women in Britain.* London: Zed Books.

Winn, S. and Stevenson, R. (1997) 'Student Loans: are the Policy Objectives being Achieved?', *Higher Education Quarterly* 51 (2): 144-163.

Wright, C. (1987) 'School Processes: An Ethnographic Study', in J. Eggleston., D. Dunn and A. Purewal. (eds.) *Education for Some.* Stoke on Trent: Trentham.

Yuval-Davis, N., Anthias, F. and Kofman, E. (2005) 'Secure Borders and Safe Havens and the Gendered Politics of Belonging: Beyond Social Cohesion', *Ethnic and Racial Studies* 28 (3): 513-535.

Index

Also from Trentham

Sikh Women in England
religious, social and cultural beliefs
Satwant Kaur Rait

Satwant Kaur Rait successfully writes about Sikh women in England and illustrates the different roles a woman plays in living her own life, whilst being a wife and a mother in a foreign country. .... Reading their experiences and how they have handled difficult times gives you great faith in the true inner strength of a Sikh woman. **Gender and Education**

A timely and essential contribution to our knowledge in gender studies, that brings new insights and perspectives ... accessible and informative. **Ethnic and Racial Studies**

This is a scholarly and fascinating ethnographic study by a Sikh woman who came to England after growing up an going to university in Delhi. It illustrates the changes in the values of Sikh women in England over the years and between the migrants and British born Sikhs. Dr Rait's research subjects, all based in Leeds, come from varied backgrounds and together make up a picture of Sikh women that is transferable to England and the UK.

Published in partnership with the Department of Theology and Religious Studies, University of Leeds.

2005, ISBN 978 1 85856 353 4
212 pages, 228 x 145mm, photos, £20.99

www.trentham-books.co.uk